#BeLikeLu

CELEBRATING A LIFE WELL LIVED

Christine Richie-Bomey

David J. Brown

Copyright © April 2021

#BeLikeEd

God Bless the United States of America

#BeLikeEd

Celebrating a Life Well Lived

All rights reserved

Copyright © April 2021 DAVID J.BROWN

DAVID J.BROWN BOOKS LLC

http://www.davidjbrownbooks.com

Paperback ISBN:

Library of Congress Control Number:

Cover design by John Steinman and Angie Simonson

This book may not be reproduced, transmitted, or stored in whole or in part by any means, including graphic, electronic, or mechanical without the express written consent of the publisher except in the case of brief quotations embodied in the critical articles and reviews

.

PRINTED IN THE UNITED STATES OF AMERICA

GOD BLESS AMERICA

PUBLISHER'S NOTE

"#BeLikeEd A Life Well Lived" is the 5th in a series of novels by David J Brown.

This book and Mr. Brown's other books:

"Daddy Had to Say Goodbye"

"Flesh of a Fraud"

"Harvest Season-Body Parts"

"Altered Egos"

Are all available, free of charge through the, "United States Library of Congress National Library Services for the Blind and Physically Handicapped" as well as from the, "State of Minnesota Department of Health Services for The Blind and Handicapped."

#BeLikeEd

This story is a work of fiction. It is inspired in part, by true life events. In certain cases, locations, incidents, characters and timelines have been changed for dramatic purposes. Certain characters may be composites or entirely fictitious.

A very special thank you to:

Timothy S. Palm II of:

BIGGDOGG LEATHER

Located in Geneva, OH for your incredible loving gifts.

You are a true artist of leather, I am in your debt.

BiggDogg Leather @ https://youtu.be/mcj1tADYqXU

July 5, 2021

#BeLikeEd

Your authors thank you.

Christine Richie-Bomey

To: Kevin Cudbertson
Life is what you make it... Make it a good one!
Christine Richie-Bomey

David J. Brown

Dare to Dream my Friend

Richie-Bomey/Brown

INTRODUCTION

This writing is by far the greatest undertaking that I have ever been challenged with. I am writing about a man who I have never met and yet I know him through his many friends. The 'Ivory towered assholes of literature' would be more than happy to point out all of my many failings for not following their, "Golden Rules of Writing." I am most certain they want to challenge my definition of this book as it is being listed as a Memoir.

Because I don't look like a constipated freak, with fish hooks in my face, sporting glam multi-colored hair and tattoos with the latest political bullshit statement of the season that I am not to be taken seriously as an author. I consulted with my pals at Google for the proper definitions of, Biography vs. Autobiography vs. Memoir.

As most know, those definitions of autobiography and Memoir are written by the living and in the first person. As all things of higher education there are distinct exceptions to most all rules.

Some autobiographies are written in the third person as I've done throughout my other four books, while destroying their, "Fourth wall."

Those ivory tower fuckers don't care much for that but I don't follow their chicken shit rules. Just because you're educated, doesn't mean you get to make the rules and it sure as shit doesn't always mean that you're smart. So to avert any possible critical discussions by a learned person let me just say, "Go bite a fart!"

Of course I very much doubt that any of my writings will ever fall into their capable hands. I am writing about a friend that many (myself included) have never met. Yet we know Ed.

Edward Allen Morris has passed from this world, however he continues to be with us in spirit. I can easily state this because I see Ed's continuing gifts of validation in the eyes and hearts of most all.

No two people know the very same person in the very same way. Each and every relationship is unique unto itself. Just think back to the last time you read an obituary of someone you've known for an extended period of time or listened to a eulogy at the funeral, you will always find that there was something that you didn't know about that person.

I promised myself that I was done writing after my fourth novel was published. There was really nothing more to say. After all, these four books are my life story. My intent was to bring hope and promise to people who lived like I did and there are many of us. Sadly, so very few are willing to come to terms with themselves and perhaps just as sad is that they go throughout their lives feeling damaged and insignificant.

Again, I truly believed that I was done. I gave all I had to give, right up until a current event pulled me up short and told me that I needed to pay it forward. This event came about from my listening to my three dear friends Podcasts over the last few years. Those friends are Christine Bomey, Eric Bomey and John Solar. John is a close friend to the Bomey's and is the producer of Christine's and Eric's weekly Podcasts.

I guess my 'aha moment' or Eureka came from my training and experience as a police officer.

What I learned from being a police officer was the art of listening. I don't just listen to your words, I listen to your use of words, your tone of voice, your body language, your hand movements, your eyes and your subtle facial expressions. I also interpret your silence, I can hear everything you don't say in words and it frightens most. I trained myself further, how to listen to what's not being said and the inflection of certain words and sentence structures and how oftentimes people will breeze over one of the most important of all facts in any investigation. I believe Lewis Carroll said it best in, "Alice in Wonderland" when Alice cried out, "This makes me more curiouser and curiouser!"

In my case, what I heard John Solar 'not say' and then breeze over it as if the words were never spoken, told me everything that I needed to hear and yes, it did make me more curiouser and curiouser!

During these podcasts there are the three principles, (Eric, Christine and John) and always a few off-site panel guests along with the open chat room and a call-in-line. Everyone is well acquainted with each other and have been friends for many years. John was in the middle of doing some home improvement projects. In the past two months, John and his guests have spoken about the high cost of building materials, lack of quality lumber and overall availability. The guys were saying that six months ago an eight-foot 2x4 stud costs $1.89 and today that same stud is now near or over $10.00 each and the quality of lumber was of the lowest grades sold. John had to use steel studs as he could only find one or two eight foot straight studs in an entire bundle of lumber that all looked like hockey sticks. The guys were almost talking in code last Friday during Eric's, "Locked and Loaded" show, which brought my ears to full alert. John made a small slip-up when he said to his listening audience and fellow panel members that he was building a, "Room within a Room."

    I know John to have a great fondness in producing these Podcasts for a large group of friends throughout the world. I have been a guest several times on both Christine's and Eric shows, speaking of my books. I was able to see some of John's studio equipment, during a live video feed during one of the live podcasts. I was impressed with the quality of his studio equipment but now John is building a, "Room within a Room?" That told me he was doing only one thing, he was building his own soundproof recording studio, which explains the, "Room within a Room."

    Christine, Eric and John, along with a great number of their listening public were aware of my narrating my first book for Audiobook, the countless months I spent reading and the jubilation I felt when it was completed and ready for edit and then on to production. Then a few weeks later, I found out how the fellow I paid to record my voice screwed me. I got nothing and he stole my money. I knew at the time that people would be bothered with knowing that, but that's just one of life's things that none of us have any control over. We trust who we believe is trustworthy and in this case, my trust was poorly spent. Eric and Christine felt terrible as they recommended this slimy asshole. He is the son of Eric's childhood best friend. They had no idea of what this loser was actually all about.

    The following morning after John's 'slip-up', I went to the Bomey's home to pick up Eric to go to a local gun show. I went into their home for a few moments and asked them both (with my best piercing 'death look') and said, "What the fuck are you guys up to? And don't bullshit me!" Of course they both had the look of extreme innocence and at the same time they knew it wouldn't dance with me. That's when I said, "John's, "Room within a room" is code for him building a recording studio isn't it? Not a question my lovelies, it's a statement. Now give!"

    They both had a shocked but a knowing look that I had figured it out. Christine's only response was, "You sure won't let people get away with anything will you!" Eric of course said, "That's your cup of piss asshole, drink it!" And then they told me the story.

    The Podcast principles along with Phil (and I suspect a few others) have been gathering materials to build and supply the recording studio, much like

Squirrels busily gathering acorns. Knowing the character of those four involved you have to know that they were only going to install the very best of the best equipment. John Solar has a very melodic and professional sounding radio voice. Christine confided that John has been seeing a voice and recording coach because he wants to record all four of my books for Audiobook and he wants them to be perfect. Christine and Eric all but threatened to sit on my chest and feed me worms if I let it out of the bag. Eric had a grin as wide as his face as he lifted his shirt to expose his Smith & Wesson model 629, 44 Magnum. I took the oath of silence and we all shook on it as Eric went on to say, "There will be no more talk of this, our lips are sealed and so are yours!"

    The moment Eric and I left his home, the Hamster wheels started spinning in my brain. How in the fuck am I ever going to be able to repay this level of kindness? Things like this are not supposed to happen for people like me! Yes, I have dedicated the last thirty years of my life to help others like me. I have been writing to help others like me since 2009. My only desire is to reach people that have lost their way and their will to live. My motto in 2009 was and still is today, "If I can just reach one soul."

You would not let me go, you asked for more, you demanded it. I'm grateful for your allegiance and your kindness. I've completed this part of my journey.

Never let anyone tell you that you can't do it.
Never tell yourself that you can't do it.

Within all fiction lies a bit of the truth
Within all truth lies a bit of fiction.
Our perceptions are the deciding factors.

David J. Brown

#BeLikeEd

CHAPTER 1   THE WILD BULL BUFFALO

That is when I knew my retirement from writing was a myth. Hell, my latest book, "Altered Egos" was released just three weeks ago! I had plans for the entire summer of taking a pail of my favorite pet earthworms for swimming lessons to a few trout streams and lakes. Now Eric Bomey and I are on our way to the gun show with me driving and the hamster wheel in my head is starting to squeak. I hope I don't run this truck up a power pole or fly off the road and into the bay of Lake Superior. I knew that I had to pay it forward and I know that time is now. Through God's loving grace, I didn't kill us both on the way to the gun show. Once we arrived, the line to get into the gun show went on forever.

Hell, the line started deep out into the parking lot and snaked all through the eight sets of double doors and then up a tall staircase and all around the entire circumference of the arena auditorium. This was the first gun show in the state since Covid hit, a year and a half ago. Eric and I just had a bit of small talk with a few people around us in line. We went there just to look around a bit and visit with our friend Craig Lawrey, who owns Hammerdown Firearms and is an FFL dealer who has helped Bunkie and I fill out the bulk of our collection. Craig is a straight up guy with an exceptionally vast knowledge of all things that go boom. Craig is more than fair in his pricing and trades values, he always has sixteen tables of the better to best handguns and rifles.

    The crowd was crazy around his tables, his three helpers were all doing the FBI purchase paperwork with a number of people standing in line to process their purchase paperwork. My mind was somewhere far away.

    All I did was stand back from Craig's tables and watch this dirt-bag guy and his wife trying to steal Craig's guns off his tables. This shithead was wearing a military style web belt with an empty leather double mag pouch on his left side and an empty, open top Kydex holster on his right side. I could see his wife and him using hand and head signals. She was pushing a double decker baby stroller. The lower seat actually had a small child in it, the upper deck had a bunch of clothing where the second child would be seated. This asshole kept picking up firearms from Craig's table and slid them into his Kydex holster. He acted like he was trying to see if the gun fit his holster. If it did fit, he then motioned his wife to come closer with the baby stroller so he could slide that gun under the pile of clothing. Each time he tried this move, I would step forward and clear my throat. He was watching the people behind the tables to see if anyone was watching him. He had no idea that Eric and I were behind him and watching his every move. Each time his wife would jump back with the stroller knowing I was about to jump on this shithead and drive him headfirst into the cement floor. He got real impatient with her and gave her a sideways look as if to say, "Pay attention to me" as she was trying to say, "Ah, we are about to go to jail, we are being watched!" When she finally got the message across to him they quickly disappeared.

I had three other friends there that had tables with several nice guns. I just simply walked up to the tables and said hello and spent very little time because my mind was still on this new project. The ride home wasn't much different. I wonder how many red lights or stop signs I ran through.

When I got home and told my sweetheart Heather, aka 'Bunkey' about our conversations at the Bomey house, she just sat down with a smile and said, "I know you will do it right, you are an honorable man and I believe in you!"

I was immediately off to attempt to pay proper homage to the kindness and love of these wonderful people. I also knew that Eric was greatly disappointed that his attempt to generate a leather bound book of Ed memories never came to full fruition. A gentleman named Tim, who owns 'BIGGDOGG LEATHER' in Geneva, Ohio (who describes himself as an amateur leather crafter Lol) made a gorgeous padded leather binder with hand embossed logos and lettering in Ed's honor. The binder had several blank pages for Ed's friends to write their parting thoughts which upon completion would be presented to Ed's wife, Jules. Sadly the idea was a bust thru no part of Eric's. The Covid panic that swept the nation caused everything to collapse. Eric's plan was to mail the binder to every member that requested it to write an entry and they would in turn pass it on to the next person. With the terrible nationwide postal service delays, staffing at an all-time low in the entire shipping industry and the, "Who gives a shit" attitude along with packages being treated like NFL field goal practice footballs. (Oh and before I forget, Fuck the NFL!) Sadly, Eric had to call the binder back in, to keep it safe.

At that moment I had no idea of what I was going to do with my writing but I somehow had to pay it forward. The cool thing is, that I can write about it now and by the time this book is ready for publication, I am sure that most of John's work will be complete doing the voice overs in bringing my printed books into audio books.

It was easy to core-out a central idea for the book. The listeners of Eric's and Christine's podcasts have jokingly suggested I write about the listeners and the people in the chat rooms. My joking response was always, "None of you are interesting or significant enough to write about." The truth is that they are all quite interesting people, unique may be a better word. I call them my friends, but I'm getting ahead of myself.

What I hadn't told anyone is that I am already eighty pages deep into my fifth novel. If I learned anything from my writing experiences, it was to not tell people what my plans are. While writing my last two novels, I was interrupted continuously by well-meaning people who wanted to know when it's going to be released, what it's about, could they buy the first few chapters, if there is going to be a pre-sale and on and on. I promised myself I would never fall into that trap ever again. Well, now those eighty pages are going to go into a folder and I will hold them for a later date, but right now I got bigger fish to fry.

Trying to identify a starting point, of course, leads me to the beginning. My relationship within the group and even the whole idea of defining and identifying the group is mind boggling. A well tenured college professor of Sociology from a top rated school, would pop an infant's pacifier in their mouth and open a new box of crayons, if they were charged with this daunting task. That or maybe they would just sit back deeply in their chair and have an Aneurysm!

So here I sit with questionable skills (at best) trying to gather the nerve to jump into this lion's den, while wearing pork chop shorts!

There is no clear way in my mind, of identifying this group or perhaps maybe a community is a better description than a group. So once again I have to surrender and drag myself to the authorities of all definitions, Google. My pal's at Wikipedia tell me (not so clearly) that a group is a community of a social unit. A group of living things with commonalities such as shared norms in values which has customs of identity. Communities may share a sense of place situated in a given geographical area, a country, a village, a town or neighborhood or in virtual space through communication platforms. I think that in-part would define our group. Our interests are many and are shared with a deep passion. Most all things revolve around the Constitution of the United States and our willingness to defend our country and families at all costs. Most all members of the group own or have built some of the finest firearms the world will ever see. They are nothing like you would see in a common gun shop. There's a great deal of pride in the conditions of our firearms as well as our shooting abilities. I have been on two group outings with a number of the members and to clear this up, there's no membership card, no dues or fees, or secret handshakes. We are just a group of likeminded people who carry a great deal of respect for each other. There is no room for jealousy in our circle, we don't look down on each other or what each other owns, we look out for each other, we are a family.

    On those two outings there were between eighteen to twenty people from all over the country, one member is from Scotland who just became a naturalized citizen. When everyone laid out their firearms (both handguns and long guns) it was like an open house. You could shoot anyone's firearm and everyone brought large amounts of ammunition for everyone to shoot along with paper and metal targets. I felt an even greater camaraderie with these fellows and ladies that I even felt when I was both a paramedic and a police officer. This unit or group or community or whatever the hell you want to call us, all maintain a strong level of mutual respect. Nobody is better than the next guy or gal, nobody is smarter, nobody's tougher, and nobody's richer. We stand on a common ground of God, family and country. We are just people, being good people. We are all individuals with a shared sameness. The only rules that need not be not spoken are the simple rules of all honorable men and women.

It only took me a matter of moments to identify what the core of this new book must be. The title of this book came as fast as the core idea. This book will be about our friend who has passed, Mr. Edward Allan Morris. The title of the book is, "#BeLikeEd."

I have been told that, "TheRealCobra Burnout" coined the, "#BeLikeEd" phrase. Sadly I've never met Ed, he passed away three years ago. Shortly after Ed passed I found my way into this group.

The reverence that so many spoke of in reference of Ed and the #BeLikeEd hats and T-shirts were the truest of any battle cries in celebration of their brotherhood. I called Christine and Eric and asked them if I could be a guest on this coming Friday and Saturday's live podcasts. I explained to them that I want to do a memorial, if you will, in memory of Ed and the group and to once again, attempt to pay it forward. I said my reason for wanting to be on their show was to ask people that physically knew Ed to share their remembrances. I was going to ask on both shows that people contribute from their personal experiences with Ed. I fully know of the difficulties of attempting to write a memoir involving a large group of people. From past experiences I also knew that a number of people may want to help me do the layout and review or edit it before publication. My answer would not just be a hard no, but a rather loudly spoken, HELL NO!

So I told them that I needed to have everyone enter through email their remembrances of Ed in the next ten days. I don't have the time for phone calls to do interviews. If they miss the ten day window it won't go in the book. Both Eric and Christine agreed (as I knew they would) and thought it was a great idea and were excited about having me on their shows. Of course I can't let John Solar know that I know what he's up to, so now I find myself having to play a spin-off of, 'Mad Magazine's, Spy vs. Spy!'

Our plan was that I was to go to their home, Friday and Saturday night to do the live Podcasts. Then the shit hit! I rarely (if ever) lie or even fib to Bunkie about anything but I did last weekend and when she found out, she was in flames!

I was sitting on the deck Sunday afternoon listening to Eric's Brew review Podcast from the day before. As he was talking about him and I going to the gun show in Carlton, Minnesota.

Well, I fibbed Bunkie when she asked me how many people were wearing masks and I answered, "Almost everyone was masked." Bunkie was inside working on her computer doing work stuff. She came out to the deck for a smoke. Just as she lit her cigarette, Eric was saying, "Me and Dave Brown went to a gun show in Carlton and almost no one there was wearing masks." I lowered my head in knowing that I'm about to become a dead man. Bunkie is very cautious about being in public with this whole Covid thing. When she comes home from work she diligently washes herself, sanitizes her cellphone, her briefcase, her purse, her travel mug and her small thermos. This Covid thing is by no means a game to her and the truth is because of my being 18 years her senior she's fearful that I would catch Covid and of course, I would die.

So I could see Bunkie's' tail feathers smoldering and I knew she was going to go back inside and design her attack plan. Later that evening Bunkie very forcefully said, (which is uncharacteristic of her) "You will not attend the Bomey's Podcast in their home! You know I love them both and you also know that they are out in public on a regular basis and they both have different ideas about covid and the effects." I admitted to her as well as myself that she's not wrong and yes, I am oftentimes careless in protecting myself. The only place I've ever gone since Covid hit was either to the gas station or the grocery store. I have not socialized with anyone other than the Bomey's on a rare occasion and just the two gun shows I've been to in the last year and half. That and just the night before I spoke to our dear friend Sean Carrigan in Colorado, who's going to come out on June 8th and spend a few weeks with us. Well, Bunkie simmered down after an extended period of time. I told her that I would cancel my appointments with the Bomey's and call Sean and ask him if he couldn't wait until a later part of the year when this Covid thing dies down. I don't think it's a good idea for him to be on two airplanes and have to go through two airports and have him in our home. I felt bad about having to tell my friends that I couldn't see them or have Sean come to visit but I do have a responsibility to protect my home, Bunkie and our three fur babies. The Bomey's took it well and they fully understood. After I phoned Sean, he too understood but I still had lingering thoughts.

How the hell am I going to get this information to the people of what my needs are? I will just have to rely on the Bomey's to plead my case and get people involved with their memories of Ed, so I can continue on with this book. Then last night (Thursday) Eric (via text) asked if we had some kind of Wi-Fi set up.

He knows that I have very little knowledge of anything about computers or operating systems.

I own a ten year old ASUS laptop that I have used to write my four books on, but I understand very little about the programs and the operating systems overall. A few of my readers would be more than happy to point out that I don't even know how to use spell check properly!

#BeLikeEd

CHAPTER 2   COMING CLEAN

Eric sent me an email with a link and Bunkie jumped on her computer and they had me live in minutes. In just a few minutes of conversation, John told me that he knows that I know of the secret recording studio build. I had suspected that early on, as the Bomey's have been trusting and loyal friends with John for almost eight years.

John told me about the secret recording studio project and their plans and timelines. It set me deep back in my chair while listening to John explain how their building this sound proof recording studio was all but mind boggling, more than that, all I heard were dollar signs, lots and lots of dollar signs. We four talked for a full two hours. I thoroughly enjoyed our conversations and I learned a lot about John and his other interests. This guy is mega multi-faceted, yes a true Brainiac that not only thinks but also does! Then there's me, just an ordinary everyday Jabroni with little purpose and little interest in anything not related to the TV show Gunsmoke or firearms. Now I'm lying awake thinking how in Christ's name am I going to pay all of this forward. The answer was there right in front of me. Ed Morris! Ed was all about brotherhood and fellowship. Ed was a great promoter and believer in Justin's Final Mission, which is a fundraising effort that builds cabins in the Ozarks for returning veterans who are experiencing PTSD and other difficulties with engaging in society. This is all about reducing the suicide rate of the twenty-two plus suicides of military veterans each day, every day. Well that's certainly something I've been behind all along. I have always enjoyed conversations with John, but this night was different. I felt a kinship far beyond our base friendship, I found a purpose of heart that reaches far beyond physical handshakes.

So now its Friday mid-morning, I'm going to be a guest on Eric's show tonight, "Locked and Loaded" and I am going to announce that I want no proceeds from the audio recording for the first ninety days of this new book release, "#BeLikeEd." I would like any and all money realized to go into recouping the principal's costs of building this recording studio. If they are not comfortable with that, then perhaps donate the money to, "Justin's Final Mission" in Ed's name.

If any of you ever had the privilege of travelling to the Western States and visited their many national parks or wildlife sanctuaries with abundant wildlife, you certainly must have seen at some point, a wild buffalo. Wild free roaming Buffalo can weigh as much as 3,000 or more pounds and be as big as a pick-up truck! I had an opportunity several years ago to be trout fishing in a small stream in one of our national parks in Montana. I was working my fly rod in thigh deep water. I suddenly heard a snorting sound behind me. I looked over my shoulder and less than thirty yards away was a wild bull buffalo looking directly at me. He looked like a Greyhound bus and I felt like a field mouse. This being a National Park, I of course was not allowed to carry a firearm, which is one of the few times that I will go anywhere without a sidearm. I know enough about wild animals of that size that you cannot outrun them, if you try, they'll stomp you into dust. Not wanting to be reduced to a small pile of oozing goo seeping into the sandy soil, I took my line in and slowly walked along the edge of the river hoping that the buffalo would leave me in peace. After thirty yards of slow walking along the river's edge, I entered the dark timber and double-timed my way back to my truck and left the area.

This is what it seems like in trying to identify this book, it's a huge wall of snot slinging, fire breathing beasts. Where do I find the common ground to write about this group and what they've done for me?

My beginning goes back to more than 50 years ago to where I met Eric's mother when Eric was seven or eight years of age. Eric's mother worked at the same ambulance service that I worked at. She worked her full time job as a R.N. at one of our local hospitals, in the emergency room. She did our insurance billing at night and ran road trips on her days off. Her being a single mother, she had to bring her children along with her in the evening. Eric was one of her children. The kids slept on the couches in the squad room watching TV. They were shy and sweet kids. The crew members always kept animal crackers, candy and chips in their lockers for them and some of us guys worked puzzles with them and read their books to them. There were also a number of highly contested games of checkers and Parcheesi with the children.

After I left the ambulance service I moved to the Western States for the next forty years of my life. When I returned to Duluth a number of events took place and I found myself reunited with Eric's mom Kathy, over coffee with a mutual friend of ours. I gave Kathy a copy of my first book. Kathy emailed me a few weeks later with her appreciation of the gift of the book and the kind words I spoke of her, her two children and Carl in that book. It was the week before Easter when Kathy invited me for lunch. Kathy invited me to enjoy lunch with her and her two adult children and their spouses. Eric of course was one of her adult children.

During our lunch I noticed Eric was wearing a firearm under his T-shirt. He is not a tall man but he is a large framed fellow, mostly all muscle and bone but I couldn't help but see the imprint of his sidearm. I made the comment to him that he was painted. He smiled as he said, "That's the way it is." I turned so he could see my firearm under my shirt. For some reason we both knew that we were about to become long term friends.

During lunch he told me that he did YouTube videos on both firearms and craft beer. He also hosted a podcast called 'Locked and Loaded' every Friday night at 8pm Central time. His wife Christine did YouTube and podcasts where she hosts a show called, "Mz.BomeyZone" on Spreaker and iHeart radio that airs live on Saturday nights at 8pm Central time. They gave me the channel addresses and I listened to the shows for a month or so. Bunkie and I went shooting with the Bomey's on several occasions and had a great deal of fun. Eric's knowledge of firearms was quite impressive. Not only that, but his firearms were just as impressive. We started having dinner weekly at a local restaurant and enjoyed their company greatly. Bunkie and I listen to both of their shows each week. We join them and their friends in the live chat rooms. This group consists of like-minded Conservatives who have a deep respect and passion for the Constitution and the American way of life.

There can and will be no question as to this group's loyalty to the Constitution of the United States and our Military Veterans. The group will have nothing to do with vigilante or left wing nut-job groups.

Now that I have returned from my mental side trip, it's time I speak of my life experiences with loss and grief while waiting for the group members' remembrances of Ed Morris. As I think about grief and loss, I can't help but think back on my own life. As a child I related to song lyrics that have carried me through the many hard times. I oftentimes, listen to Solomon Burke's song, "Cry to Me" that was recorded in 1962. A lot of artists have recorded that song but none of them carried their inner soul through the song. I wish I could add those lyrics and other lyrics of "Tears For Fears" songs, but the lawsuits for copyright infringements by some slime ball lawyers prevents that.

I don't get to back-away from my own experiences, but yet I can't let any part of this be about me, as I have never met or corresponded with Ed.

Although my life has been heavily laden with loss I have absolutely no experience with grief, it was just too painful for me. I used my pains to justify my rage until someone suggested that my rage wasn't truly warranted, but my grief was.

This brings me to having to Google for the definitions of loss and grief. Any writer with half a brain knows not to trust what they believe the definitions of words are and must research each 'topic word' to protect their credibility as a legitimate writer. It didn't take long for me to realize that grief and loss actually carry two separate meanings. My dust covered, yellowed paged, three pound dictionary, didn't give as clear a definition as my pals at Google did.

The short definition of grief is; a natural response to loss, it might be the loss of a loved one, a relationship, a pregnancy, a pet, a job or a way of life. Other experiences of loss can be due to children leaving home, infertility and separation from friends and family. The more significant the loss, the more intense the grief is likely to be. Grief is expressed in many different ways and it can affect every part of your life, your emotions, thoughts and behaviors. Grief, oftentimes, will affect your belief system, your physical health, your sense of self and identity, and relationships with others. Grief could leave you feeling sad, angry, anxious, shocked, regretful, relieved, overwhelmed, isolated, irritable or numb. Grief has no set pattern. Everyone experiences grief differently. Some people may grieve for weeks and months, while others may describe their grief lasting for years. Through the process of grief, however, you began to create new experiences and habits that work around your loss. Getting through (notice that I won't say, getting over) grief and loss is something that takes time to work through. A real friend would never tell you to get over it, a real friend will help you to get through it. Everyone will find their own way to grieve. It's important to have the support of friends and family or someone else to talk about your loss when you need to. No one gets to decide someone else's grief. Sometimes losing a pet can be as painful as losing a human.

Grief and depression are quite different but they can appear similar as they can both lead to feelings of intense sadness, insomnia, poor appetite and weight loss.

Depression stands out from grief as being more persistent, with constant feelings of emptiness, despair and a difficulty feeling pleasure or joy.

If you notice that depression symptoms continue or your grief begins to get in the way of how you live, work, share relationships or day-to-day living, then it's important to get support from professional help.

As the shock of loss fades, there is a tendency on the part of the griever to feel more pain and sadness. Well-meaning friends may avoid discussing the subject due to their own discomfort with grief or their fear of making the person feel bad. As a result, people who are grieving often feel more isolated or lonely in their grief.

People who are grieving are likely to fluctuate between wanting some time to themselves and wanting closeness with others. They may want someone to talk to about their feelings.

Grief is part of the process of healing. It's important to note that the grief process is not linear, but it's more often experienced in cycles. Grief is sometimes compared to climbing a spiral staircase or things could look and feel like you are just going in circles, yet you are actually making progress. Being patient with the process and allowing yourself to have any feelings about the loss can help.

The length of the grief process is different for everyone. There are no predictable schedules for grief. Although it can be quite painful at times, the grief process should not be rushed. It is in fact a process and it's important to be patient with yourself as you experience your unique reactions to loss. With time and support, things generally do get better. However it is normal for significant dates, holidays or other reminders to trigger feelings related to the loss. Taking care of yourself, seeking support and acknowledging your feelings during these times are ways that could help you cope.

Sudden or shocking loss due to events like crimes, accidents, or suicide can be quite traumatic. There's no way to prepare. They can challenge your sense of security and confidence in the predictability of life. You may experience symptoms such as sleep disturbance, nightmares, distressing thoughts, depressed mood, social isolation, or severe anxiety.

Predictable loss like those due to terminal illness, sometimes allow more time to prepare for the loss. However, they create two layers of grief: the grief related to the anticipation of the loss and grief related to the loss itself.

CHAPTER 3 MISERY HAS A GUN

As many others have, I too have experienced most all of the emotions described in the descriptions of grief, loss and depression. In one five sentence paragraph the word, 'process' was mentioned four times. As in all things of life, process is imperative.

For me, I have been taught through life's cruelties, that all living things do not come with a timestamp nor is there an expiration date. As I sit here now in this writing, I must ask myself if I made a difference. Will I be remembered? Will I be missed?

I regretfully have had multiple experiences both as a child, as a young man and throughout my adult life with death, both personal and witnessed, viewing death and living with death. My first memories of grief came to me at age four. My older brother Donnie (6 yoa) was admitted to the University of Minnesota Hospital to die. Donnie lived there for three years. My family lived 150 miles away. We drove to the hospital to visit him every Sunday unless my dad had to work or there were snow storms. Donnie was there all alone, sometimes for weeks without seeing anyone other than the people in white smocks. There were times that I wished he would die so he would not have any more pain and have to be all alone. Other times I wished he would die so my mom and dad wouldn't be so sad. If they weren't so sad and mean, maybe they would stop beating me.

I think I was nine or ten years old when my grandfather's wife died. Her name was Esther. She was a very nice lady, actually we were buddies, and we had secrets. She let me smoke and drink hot chocolate with her in her kitchen when I was shoveling snow at their house. I called her 'E' when we talked.

When 'E' was hospitalized with bone cancer I visited her every day, sometimes twice a day for several weeks. Her death greatly affected me because she was my first adult friend. My take-away of that experience was not to allow myself to get to like people too much. Even at that time, I wondered how people could be so indifferent when people die. My grandpa and my parents didn't seem all that affected by her passing. I was confused and angry about that. I guess that was my first life lesson in denying your pain. In my young years, I witnessed a great deal of death. Waiting and praying for my brother's death was emotionally and spiritually paralyzing. My family could only pray and wait, all things of normalcy were on hold. There were no smiles, no laughter and no joy. There was always a gasping dread when the phone rang, fearing that the hospital was calling to tell us that Donnie was gone. As time passed Donnie became better and was able to finally come home. I tried to be happy but I remember the doctor said that there were no guarantees and Donnie could die at any time. I clearly remember Donnie coming home and all my aunts, uncles and cousins came to our apartment and had gifts, cake and ice cream. I couldn't allow myself to celebrate as they did. I lost my faith in god and medicine, I was certain that they sent him home to die.

My grandmother (my mom's mother) was a slutty whiskey pig. She intentionally burnt my right hand badly and I wanted was to kill her and then kill myself.

I saw my young friend's dead body being carried from the water and witnessed two men drown all before I was twelve years old. I was always sad and lonely. I thought it would be better if I died right then, rather than having to live in my loneliness for the rest of my life.

I buried my baby girl just as I completed the eleventh grade of high school. I of course was heartbroken. The only advice I received was from my mom when she said, "You kids are young, you can have more children later on." Within four months of my baby girl's death, my wife left me for another man. I couldn't allow myself to feel that pain. I had to turn my loss of my baby and wife into something external. I was beyond angry, I was full of rage and I declared that I would never care about anyone, ever again.

Before I graduated from high school, I found myself standing before a judge in divorce court. That is when I took my silent oath to never allow myself to get, 'too happy'. What surprises me in those last few pages of definitions of loss and grief, was that nowhere in those dictionary definitions did I find any mention of God or Spirituality. I believe that Google missed the mark by a country mile. I have yet to know anyone who hasn't been angry with God for taking their loved one too soon, or for allowing them to suffer for so long. I don't believe I ever witnessed a loss where someone didn't cry out with their pain and bewilderment of God's presence or lack thereof.

    Several people that have read my first novel, "Daddy Had to Say Goodbye" asked if any of those stories were true. My answer is always the same, "Although my books are all listed as novels, the only fiction in my first book were the locations and persons names. Yes, I witnessed all of that sorrow as a paramedic and I still carry that pain. I have learned how to live with it.

    There is a cruel and brutal awakening, when someone who is dying grabs for your hand with great effort, then begs you not to let them die, as you watch their life leave them and become just another dead body. It doesn't matter who you are, that changes you and it changes you forever. It wasn't just watching people die, it was holding them as they died.

    Many patients (full well knowing they were dying) would ask me to tell their family members that they were truly sorry for their mistakes and failings in life, the pleading in their eyes made me promise that I would pass along those messages, which I did, each and every time. There is one situation that visits me almost every day of my life.

An eight year old boy who was hit by a car was pinned underneath and was dragged for several yards. He knew even in his young years that he was dying. I crawled under the car to hold him as fire rescue was trying to lift the car off of him. I had to make sure that none of his limbs were entangled in the undercarriage of the car as they lifted the car off of him. He was taking shallow breaths and was semiconscious with him taking only eight shallow breaths a minute. His eyelids fluttered open, he looked directly into my eyes and my soul at the same moment as he said, "Please tell my little sister Sally, that she can have my turtle." And that.... was his final breath.

Some days I think of those few moments with that little boy and it leaves me thinking that that event placed the dagger in my heart, other days I see the purest of selfless love. The love of his turtle and the love of his little sister.

I didn't ask anyone his name that day, because I already knew his name, his name is Angel. He is my Angel. He keeps me right sized. He and a few others are the total sum of why I continue to write and try to reach people like me.

On the dark days that I felt that dagger plunging into my heart, my only defense mechanism was denial as to how it all affected me. That and alcohol. Alcohol and women were my safe place and that safe place was a lie and I knew it. I used booze and women to deflect the reality in my gut.

I tried to run from my pain but it was like I was handcuffed to a treadmill without an off switch. I had to keep running to avoid capture. I had to stay ahead of my misery because my misery…...had a gun!

CHAPTER 4 DEMONS KILL

Most all people want to believe that they could withstand the feared, "Trial by fire." Damn few however, realize that you must first be immersed in those flames. Some flames burn hotter and larger than others, some produce a catastrophic infernal, if not rapidly extinguished. Some will take your life, others will cause us to give our life. We all have our heartaches and disappointments, we also can choose to make those things be our excuse or make those same things be our motivation. It's all about choices and we all get to make them.

When I think of radical life choices, driven by pains of the heart, my mind always brings me back to Robin Williams. My earliest memories of Robin were when I saw his first appearance on the Johnny Carson Show. I believe it was the same time that the television show, "Mork and Mindy" was in its first season in 1978. What I saw in Robin Williams was a sickening suicide in progress. His demons were controlling him like a marionette. It took until August 11, 2014 that his demons finally took him. He had great wealth, he had fame, he was loved by millions but he never found himself. Robin spoke in a very guarded secret code. His many statements like, "People don't fake depression...they fake being okay. Remember that. Be kind." He also said, "I think the saddest people always try their hardest to make people happy. Because they know what it's like to feel absolutely worthless and they don't want anyone else to feel like that."

I broke his code long before I ever really knew anything about him. He spoke to me, he spoke directly to me. What did I hear him say? I clearly heard him say, "I am sinking and I don't have the energy or the desire to swim. Save yourself, stay out of the water until you WANT to swim!"

Depression is a cruel mistress that wants to watch you destroy yourself. Sadly and much like Robin Williams, all the tragedies in my life (mentioned earlier) never came to an end. They continued throughout most all of my adult life. When I did finally leave police work there was a brief respite but then the dreams came and the memories came along with the dreams. Those dreams became screams, I couldn't turn in any direction as they were still there, always still there. I couldn't tell the woman I cared about, for fear of them seeing me as weak. When I had one-night-stands, I could not let myself fall asleep because I knew I would have night terrors, cry out and wake up drenched in sweat. My five wives each told me the following mornings, of my restlessness and flailing. In most cases, they were kind enough to never ask me about the names or locations that I talked about in my sleep. I think they each thought those demons would leave me at some point, much to my dismay, my demons lasted longer than all five of my marriages, combined. I just lived in a whirlwind of memories, tragic, tragic memories.

I couldn't deal with my depression and of course I never allowed myself the opportunity to grieve for any loss because I didn't have the courage. My multiple marriages, my several jobs that I was discharged from, were just simple indicators as to how badly broken I was and how dishonest I was with myself and the people around me. I was never a victim in any of these things, I was without faith and I was without courage.

I couldn't face the very demons that were trying to kill me. I would stand toe to toe with any man regardless of the size and I would be absolutely fearless. Yet when it came to my emotions, I was a coward. The guilt I carried was never truly mine to own. I felt ashamed that I didn't make the difference that I expected myself to. I had to be a hero in all people's minds so I could be comfortable with myself. Of course that never happened either.

The only true constant in my life was rage and fear. The fear once again was not about injury, it was about being found out. It was about being discovered by the people that cared for me. How does a man tell people that he was afraid to keep going, that he was a fraud and his life was worthless and of no value. I was disgusted with myself knowing full well that any woman I was in contact with, would pay the ultimate price, I would break their hearts. I wanted so desperately to love and yet I didn't know how to. I couldn't accept love from others because I couldn't trust it. Like everyone else, they too, would be gone and once again, I would be alone.

My salvation came in the early morning hours of August 7th, 1991. I came out of an alcohol induced blackout with my duty weapon in my mouth. I knew that at that very moment that either I pulled the trigger now, or I must change my life, all of my life and change it forever. That was the beginning of my lifelong journey that I'm still enjoying almost thirty years later and at this very moment.

Of course not everyone suffers from alcoholism and depression but pain and loss take many people into the frozen land of inactivity, where they now sit and wait and want to die. Some people are ashamed of trying to move on after the loss of a loved one. They may think that they are disrespecting their memories, if they smile or laugh or go anywhere that might shame themselves and the family. That paralyzing fear of, "What will people think", is a common thought amongst most all who survive and suffer loss.

Many religions and nationalities have established timelines and rituals along with dress codes for mourning.

Hell, I hope that my funeral is full of jokes, laughter and Hawaiian shirts and dresses, really short, short dresses! I want to be buried in my ten foot, trout fishing kayak. Bunkie has already told many of our friends that there would be a cover charge to enter the mortuary (because more than a few mourners want to make sure I'm dead) and for an additional twenty bucks, you can enter the, "Share the pot" like they do in the bingo parlors. I want caged Go-Go girls, dancing to the 'Ventures' doing the Frug, the Watusi, the Locomotion, the Pony, the Boogaloo, the Jerk, and the Stroll, with the music played on speakers like the deep gut sound of the 1957 Fender Stratocasters with reverb. I want music crankin out from Elvis, Dion, Johnny Rivers (his song, "The Seventh Son" of 1965 cracks me the fuck up)! The song is about every male teen's ego with them thinking "I'm the one," because they bagged a babe with their striking good looks, charm, wit, poise, grace and their star-like smooth dance moves. That guy was me!

    As teenagers we were all tripping over our dicks trying to get laid. We took them to a movie, then for a burger and a malt and sometimes after that we even took them to a Friday night dance at the Duluth Armory, to see a local band. We spent a full week's pay on a hope and a prayer that we would, "Get Some!" The winter months brought the bigger bands to town. Hell, just the admission price, caused me to drive around all week with only gas fumes in the tank!

    In 1959 I took a babe to the annual "Winter Dance Party" starring: Buddy Holly, Ritchie Valens, Dion and "The Big Bopper", J.P. Richardson, at the Duluth Armory. With the price of those tickets there was no chance of any pre or after food stops and I should have been able to have banged her, her two sisters and her mom!

Three days later, the men on the billboard (excluding Dion) were all gone in a fiery plane crash in Clear Lake, Iowa. That day, February 3rd 1959 is still known today as, "The Day the Music Died."

I want full wall videos of the "Second Hand Lions" bar fight, some Clint Eastwood stuff with him asking, ".......well do ya punk?" And a shitload of John Wick flicks of him double tapping his way to fame! I hope Bunkie will hire our pal Craig Lawrey from Hammerdown Firearms to cater the event with his world famous, 'Ketchup' sandwiches.

Oh yes and one more thing, in lieu of flowers I would like my female mourners to wear colorful bras and matching panties to be removed in front of me and fill my kayak fishing casket. I want Bunkie to have a bouquet of flowers in her hand, face my body and turn her back to the 'kinda-sorta' mourners, then throw those flowers over her shoulder as she shouts, "Whoever catches these is next!" I also hope when people speak of me that they start their sentences with, "That fuckin guy..........." or…….. "You won't believe this shit………!"

CHAPTER 5 FAME IS A TRAP

I'm still waiting for some of the members of the group to submit their memories of Ed Morris. I actually researched the mechanics of writing a memoir as I have no experience in that area. Many if not most all established writers, shy away from anything that requires input from others. I have had several people ask (some even begged) me to write their life stories. I know people too well, so as not to step in that bear trap. Some expected me to spend countless hours and days on the phone with them so I could write their story like, "As told to the author by……"

Some were so intense that they wanted me to travel several states away so I could interview them in the comfort of their own home so I could better understand them and see the depth of their soul through their eyes. Then there were the ones who wanted to come to my home for inspiration, thinking that they could somehow 'catch' what I have just from being where, "The Magic happens." Of course none of those people had any money (even for my travel expenses) but they all said that they would give me a percentage of their book sales. When I told them that there was a cost to the writer for production, they somehow just thought that I would take care of that little matter. I gave them the list of costs just for the cover design and photography and followed that up with the universal average total sales for an independent published author is under $500.00 (in a good year and with a large fan base). I instantly became the asshole of the century for crushing their dreams. The arguments were many with some saying that JK Rowling's was an independent writer and today she is super rich! Some promised a higher percentage of sales commissions or other creepy enticements that were laughable at best, it just seemed to never end.

    I have an elderly neighbor (four years my senior) who strolls twice-a-day through the neighborhood to stay in shape and always waves but we have never spoken. One day as I was mowing the lawn, he stopped me and asked me what I did for a living. I told him that I was retired but I am an active novelist. He about lost his fucking mind as he tripped on his own tongue with telling me that he too was a writer, so we started the conversation that eventually gave him cause to hate my guts. Come to find out the poor guy was only a dreamer. I took a break from lawn mowing and invited him to come up and sit on the deck. I got us both a bottle of ice water as I explained to him (from my experience) what the writing industry is truly about and what it takes to get published. His eyes became wider and wider and even wider when I told him about the ugliness and the circling sharks in the water in this industry. I went in the house and brought out my three (at the time) currently published novels, signed and handed them to him. I thought he was going to lose consciousness, he was amazed that I actually had written and published three novels and lived in the same city block as him. I could see the bile building in his throat when he realized that he was just dreaming. He had no idea of the amount of work and costs it takes to write and publish a book. Of course I made it clear that I didn't review people's work as that is a very personal matter and that I am not an authority on anyone else's work, other than my own. The Following day he was all but skipping down the street. I was sitting on my back deck as he asked if he could join me as he was waving a standard, legal size manila envelope.

    He said in an almost childlike giddiness, "I've got my book for you to look at." Well I did look at it. It was eight, handwritten pencil and pen notebook pages. The sparkle in his eyes said that he was convinced that he was about to set the literary world ablaze. He told me that he would check back with me tomorrow as he hopped back down the road.

    None of his stuff made any sense to me. He was trying to write about his Finnish community and his church's history. I didn't understand any part of that, nothing gave a clear and concise description of anything. I suspected that he is deep into dementia. The following day, I told him that I thought his work had promise and tried to give him a great deal of encouragement, right after I laid him out flat with all of the ugliness of the publishing world. He now thinks he might want to raise Chinchilla's or Mink or some kind of fucking little rat. That was a year and a half ago, I see him daily but he has not spoken to me since.

There are several pitfalls in attempting to write when the author has to wait (wait being the operative word) for others input. Originally, I set a ten day window for the deadline. For three weeks I asked both Eric and Christine to announce during their shows that I needed the friends of Ed to please forward their experiences with him. Eric, Christine and John Solar all but pleaded with their listeners (who are their friends) to submit their entries so I could include them in the book. Two of the members who were personal friends of Ed, stonewalled me. I texted and called them both. One said he would do it right away, the other never took my call or answered my text. I got nothing from either. One of my supposed gifts is that I understand people quite well, sometimes all too well.

Some people feel empowered when they know someone is waiting and counting on them. Almost as though they hold power over someone. Not with me however, I worked my ass off to develop my power and my power belongs to me!

Part of their supposed power is to keep me guessing why they blew me off. I don't give any part of a fuck what their reasons are but I suspect it has to do with a propped up ego. I had two people ask if I would call them and do a phone interview with them. I said, "No I don't write someone's or anyone's story and I won't write yours. Neither of those two submitted anything.

During a phone call between my sweetheart, 'Bunkie' along with Christine, they asked what I think about these people not submitting their experiences. My answer was delivered with a grin. "Ladies, the reasons are as many as there are fish in the sea. Some people are afraid of being misunderstood. Some don't want to expose themselves and their inability to write. Some can't come to grips with their loss. I have heard my own family voice their anger toward my dad who died from lung cancer at the age of 50, because he smoked. Some may be angry because I'm writing about Ed and I had never met him. Perhaps some may think that I am going to profit off of Ed's death when I sell the book. Some of this bullshit has to do with simple jealousy. I know of one former member (who I attempted to contact) who is a classic Narcissist. I think he may have written the book, "The Beginners Guide to Narcissism." With the subtitle of, "How to be a Dick!"

The mental health professionals might very well have studied him to form the description of Narcissism. Narcissists don't want honesty or sharing friendships. They want people to celebrate them. They demand blind loyalty and you must always take their side in all matters. If you challenge them or disagree on any level, you will be damned to the flames of hell. They blame others for their own failings as nothing is ever their fault. Lastly, they will go to great lengths to destroy you. They most often times talk louder than anyone else and interrupt others as well as talk over most all other people. They will broadcast to all, how you wronged them and oftentimes they will include savage and spiteful threats of bodily harm. My experience tells me that the loudest person in any group is the most insecure. They use a loud voice and foolish brag to secure their position as the alpha member. I have been around many people like that over the years. My response is always to openly laugh when they try to inject their will. You can watch the steam leave them like a leaking balloon. Sometimes I will sit quietly (to intentionally draw them out to challenge me) and it unnerves them and they will ask me why I'm so quiet. That is the "Golden Moment" when I will respond with, "I'm not being quiet, I am measuring you." The loudmouthed assface all but evaporates and quietly leaves the area. Probably to go kick their dog.

CHAPTER 6   BLESSED BEYOND MY DREAMS

      I had only six letters from Ed's friends at this point and not enough to start this part of the book yet. I was disappointed for sure. Hell, the truth was that I was pissed off, but I still had hopes for the following weekend.

      The truth of it all is, I am writing this book to help the members of this group but mostly Ed's wife, Jules, to recover and heal from the loss of Ed. I don't always care to put out the truths of my heart. I know that Jules, Eric, Christine and John dearly miss Ed. John had never met Ed but they had plans to spend some time together in the forest and mountains in the very near future. John shared a number of memories of his and Ed's almost daily phone calls and texts. John told me how much he regretted waiting too long for their first time getting-together. With my life experiences I easily understood when John said, "A regret is something that can never be changed, and all we can do is learn from it." John went silent for a few minutes which told me that he had learned from it.

      On Saturday Eric, Christine, Bunkie and I went to the shooting club to make some noise. We all needed to shake off the bullshit of the world and try to breathe again. We all breathed deeply after three uninterrupted hours of blissful noise making.

I think we could have gone longer but we drained our travel mugs and thermoses of the only real coffee recommended by God. Folgers!

As we started home (Bunkie drove) I realized with a chuckle, that not one of us took our cell phones out all the time that we were at the gun range! Of course, I then immediately had to check my phone for messages. I had a message from my deceased friend's widow, Bekki Malcomson. I had tried to reach Bekki during John's latest hospitalization and his following nursing home stay. No man should die at forty-eight years of age. John Malcomson and I had plans to go on a public speaking and book signing tour this late summer. I coached John (more like kicked his ass) as he was struggling to write his book that I bullied him into writing. John had a message that all the world needed to hear. John had a dissecting aorta that almost killed him. He had a lengthy hospital stay with several surgeries and an extended home recovery period. That is when he discovered my book, "Daddy Had to Say Goodbye." John emailed me with him saying that he was a Flight Paramedic and the EMS director for Hardin County, Kentucky until he fell ill. He was now rehabbing at home and found my book and asked how he could get a copy. I mailed John a signed copy that day. That is where it all started for us. We became swell pals in a very short period of time. John told me that he was reading my book to his three year old daughter (omitting all the bad words) as part of his speech therapy.

I sent Bekki a copy of my last book, "Altered Egos" that I dedicated to John's memory. The message Bekki sent was a photograph that she took of her and John's seven year old Daughter, the same child that John read to when she was three. The picture was of seven year old Adalyn holding a framed picture of her daddy and her showing him in heaven, that a man put daddy's name in a book.

I wished at that moment that I was home alone. I didn't speak of it on the drive home, I just stared out the side window and bit down on my lower lip. When we got home I found some things to do in the garage for a few hours before I was ready to show Bunkie the picture and speak of it. Bunkie put her arms around me with her own wet eyes and said, "John would be so happy and proud of you for reaching out to his baby and giving her a piece of her daddy to carry for all of her life."

We went out to the deck and sat in silence with a cup of coffee and a few cigarettes. Bunkie kissed me goodnight and went to bed early. Her loving heart told her that I needed some quiet and alone time.

I sat on the deck alone for three hours to finally allow myself to grieve both my loss of John and our shared dream tour. As I stood up to go in the house the tears finally came, the tears were not for me but for John's suffering and his precious little Adalyn having to grow-up without her daddy.

I'm now glad that I wrote my fourth book and dedicated it to John as well as including three chapters about John. It was about telling the world about an incredible man that not only fought the good fight to recover but to bring his fight to others who needed to trust that they could fight their own good fight. Seeing that photo of that darling little girl connecting her heart with daddy was my payday. She will have that book for all of her life and can visit with it and her daddy at any time. Memories will in time fade for her as they do for all of us. The pages of books may yellow but the printed words never fade.

Today I feel both my blessings and my purpose. After twelve years of writing, fighting off my demons and believing that my work was just a foolish man's dream,
I finally found my true worth. It took the death of a dear friend and his darling little girl to show me that I have not lived my life in vain. Today, and at this very moment, as I strike these keys, I can smile and say out loud to the world that my life was and still is worth living. It's not at all about what I have received or extracted, it is and must always be about what I get to gift to others. It has finally struck me and it is here to stay this time. Today I am a good and loving man!

Oftentimes, I lose sight of the impact that my writing has on some people. I almost forgot that I wrote and published four 100,000 + word novels and that one copy of each is gathering dust on a shelf in the United States Library of Congress in our nation's capital. I can't allow my ego to consume me. It most certainly would be my end to God's most valued gift, the gift of humility. I think it was my ole friend, Casey Kasem that put it best (at least for me) when he closed every broadcast with, "And now, one more time, keep your feet on the ground and keep reaching for the stars."

I never actually met or corresponded with Casey Kasem but he was a friend to me. He was a friend to most all teenagers and under thirtyish rock music fans. He was even bigger than, "WolfMan Jack." Casey was a radio and TV Disk Jockey. He broadcast to more than one thousand stations. Casey was also a voice-over artist and was the voice of "Shaggy" in Scooby Doo as well as several children's cartoon series, including Sesame Street and the Transformers. Casey was very generous with his time and money with supporting several local and national charities. He was an annual guest on the Jerry Lewis telethon supporting Muscular Dystrophy. Casey Kasem was a grateful and humble man who proudly stated, "I'm just the guy next door" He died with an estimated wealth between $80 and $100 million dollars.

As I was writing this last paragraph, I received a phone call from my Facebook friend of five years, Kevin Cudbertson of England UK. This is the first time that we have spoken. We are mutual fans of each other. Kevin was a submarine driver for the English Navy for eighteen years. His ship did several joint naval exercises with the US Navy. Kevin's first time ashore on US soil was at Norfolk VA. His first experience with American food was a Hostess Twinkie and he loved it!

#BeLikeEd

      Kevin felt a calling to better serve mankind and left the Navy to become a Paramedic. Kevin is now a Senior Paramedic and FTO (Field Training Officer) and works with the new hires just out of Paramedic school. Kevin is an avid if not rabid reader. I don't remember who friend requested who, but I received a message from Kevin requesting info on where he could find my books. Because Kevin was a Professional Paramedic and his fb profile, along with several of his posts, I easily saw a gentle and caring man dedicated to service of those in desperate need. It was my pleasure to gift and sign a copy of my first two books, "Daddy Had to Say Goodbye" and "Flesh Of a Fraud " to him. Kevin received my books after three weeks of package hockey at the post offices of the US and the UK.

      It was a few weeks after Kevin received my books that he sent me a lengthy email. Kevin was over the top with his compliments on my writing. He said he thought at times he was reading the works of Frank McCourt the Nobel Prize winner for writing "Angela's Ashes" and at other times it felt like he was reading, "Bar Fly" by Charles Bukowski. I found that to be quite flattering and a bit amusing because I never read either of those books and I didn't know those authors names. Since that time I have had more than a few readers make very similar claims which pushed me to Google those two book titles but I was careful not to go beyond the basic overview of each book. I avoid reading anything that will even remotely seep into my mind and potentially influence my writing. I don't need any outside influence to sway me in any direction. I write my story, my way and nobody else's. If I do read, I read trash westerns.

I have never read any of the "Greats" of literature. I used to read police novels twenty years ago but since then I have very little time to read. I'm a writer, I write, it's what I do.

As our phone conversation began, Kevin was wanting to ask where I developed my writing skills and who I studied under. If I dedicated certain times of each day to write and if I had a minimum daily word count goal. If I was a member of a writing group and about a dozen other rapid-fire questions. I all but pissed myself laughing as I dropped my voice to 'police command orders' when I told him to shut up and listen.

I said, "Kevin, I'm just a guy who told a story on paper. I wrote my second book to prove to myself and the rest of the world that I wasn't just a 'one-trick pony'. I looked at my two published books several times each day. I was overwhelmed with God's loving grace that showed me the way and reason to write. My third book was a continuum of the story line of my life story. My fourth book was driven by the pain of losing two people that were deep in my heart and who were taken from us all, much too soon.

My writing group consists of three Papillion's fur babies and we meet twenty-four hours a day, seven days a week. I don't have a daily writing schedule or word count goal. I am untrained and most of the time, undisciplined. I write when and what I want, when I want to. I have no contractual demands or no boss. Except for my sweetheart 'Bunkie' of course. She asks very little of me as far as household chores, she wholly supports my writing.

You my friend, don't get free admission into my life. You must pay to play, you want something, I want something. You my swell Pal, need to write your own fucking book. Every time you post on Facebook, you and your buddies lose me with your slang talk. Not one of you dinks can write two sentences without throwing several slang words in that confuse the hell out of me. You pricks talk almost in code, like the 29 Navajo men who joined the United States Marine Corps in 1942 and served in the Pacific during World War II as radio operators. They developed an unbreakable code language using parts of their native Navajo tongue. They were known as, "The Navajo Code Talkers" and were extremely significant in protecting our troops from enemy ambushes.

Kevin promised me that he will write a glossary for me. He then rolled out his remaining list of questions.

Kevin: Where did you find the courage to step into the world of literature?

Me: I decided as a young man that I would no longer let people tell me that I wasn't good enough and I have held true to my declaration to this very day.

Kevin: What about the detractors and doubters?

Me: Fuck them!

Kevin: Do some of your readers complain about some of the colorful language you use?

Me: Fuck them too!

Kevin: I do admire your confidence but does that affect your book sales?

Me: Fuck em again!

Me: continued: Look, Kevin. My freedom from self-doubt comes from my understanding that I don't have to compare or measure-up to anyone. If you don't like my writing, don't buy my books. Your approval is not necessary for my continued writing.

Skippy, let me toss this pearl of knowledge to you. Louis Armstrong was trying to explain jazz music to a group of first year, first semester, music students at the Juilliard School of Performing Arts. After several attempts to answer many of the students' questions, Mr. Armstrong finally gave up and said, "There are some folks that, if they don't know, you can't tell em." He then left the stage without another word and walked out of the building. I think my simple answer of, "Fuck em" serves that same purpose with fewer words.

Kevin: I have to level with you on this mate. These questions that I am asking are not just my questions. You have an undeclared group of fans here in England. Actually, they are my friends. I unintentionally started your UK fan club, perhaps. I would either be at work, have friends over to the house or in the pub, and I would tell my mates and family of my reading your writing and the things I have been learning about myself. For the last four years we have been sniping you. We of course have all read your last four books. We watch your Facebook posts, we watch your comments on other people's posts. Most all of my friends and family are of the suspicion that 'David Brown' is a pen name for a famous writer who wants to write freely without the expectations that his fans will demand he follow his past work. A new beginning perhaps, David? Some of the lads (who follow conspiracy mysteries) think that you are probably a movie script editor, or even a custodian who captures discarded prose from the rubbish and uses the discards to write a super master edition of a literary jigsaw puzzle). We think that you are a genius who wants to remain anonymous. You use hard words like fuck and fuck em to keep us off your trail.

      Some of the group doesn't believe that you were a poor student. They think you are too smart to be uneducated or undereducated. You know far too much of everything, for any one of us to believe anything else. You omitted all the history of three years of your young life in, "Daddy Had to Say Goodbye" and there were a few other discrepancies of time lines throughout your life. You tore our guts to shreds in several chapters of your first book. No one doubts that you were a top notch Paramedic or even a Police Officer but again you were too smart to be, just a cop. Some of us think that you were a deep cover agent for one of the alphabet agencies that you make reference to in your writings, perhaps even you worked for another nation all together.

You sound tough as hell and nobody in our group would want to cross you, but in your posts and books, you are a hard edged teddy bear that wants the very best for all. What say you my friend?

Me: Sounds like you have a few mystery writers in your group. And no, I have never been to a writing or editing or movie studio. I am me, sorry to disappoint you blokes (if blokes is a proper word). Now what should we talk about?

Kevin: So you have no comment in all of that layout?

Me: Do you like to fish?

Kevin: That is the smartness in you! You won't talk about anything that you don't want to talk about. Nobody can ever trap you. You have had some superb training.

Me: Life has trained me, no one else. What color is your house?

Kevin: OK Mate I will leave it be.

Me: Tell me about your wife and child. Your daughter looks like she has a lot of juice and a bit of game in her.

Kevin: Our Tilly is now a 12 year old, full time giggler. Everything is funny to her and her favorite comedian is John Belushi. She can't stop laughing. She is also quite a practical joker.

I couldn't help but think of the movie, Animal House when John Belushi filled his mouth with his cheeks all but bursting with cottage cheese, slapped his cheeks with his palms and blew cottage cheese on everyone while announcing that he was a zit. I hope to hear some day that Kevin will get to enjoy that scene relived at the dining table in his own home! That will teach him to call me a faker.

    We enjoyed a few more minutes of conversation and said let's talk again soon.

CHAPTER 7 SO…WHAT ABOUT ED?

If I have learned anything at all, about the the last three years of my association with the Bomey's and this group, I have learned that there is no, "Who was Ed?" It is rather, "Who is Ed?"

From my time in conversation with Eric and Christine and John, reading the many emails from his friends, attending a few gatherings of friends of Ed, spending time and sitting with Ed's wife of forty years, Jules and watching and listening to countless hours of podcasts I have declared that Ed is an "Is."

Ed still lives very much, in the hearts and minds of many. This is why I am writing this book.

I won't allow Ed's memory to fade away with the seasons, or his crumbling headstone in the future decades to be the only marker of Ed's presence on this earth, not after all the many things he brought to people's hearts. In future generations, Ed as all the rest of us (yes we will all die too) will be nothing more than a leaf in a family tree on some website. His and our possessions will be cherished for a time, but will all be gifted, sold or simply be dropped in the trash. Books however will live on forever. Edward Allen Morris, is an 'Is', and he will always be an 'Is' for all of time.

#BeLikeEd

This is Ed's funeral notice.

IN LOVING MEMORY
Edward Allen Morris
"Ed"
March 30th 1957 - October 16th 2018
Visitation & Last Respects
Saturday, March 23, 2018
9:00am - 11:00am

The mortuary pamphlet reads:
In loving memory Edward Allen Morris
March 30, 1957-October 16, 2018
US Air Force Retiree
Originally from Tennessee and presently from Illinois, was called to his eternal rest on October 16, 2018 at the age of 60 years.
Mass of intention will be held on Friday, March 22, 2019, at Saint Jude Thaddeus Church in Sinajana at 7:00 pm.
Visitation and last respects will be held on Saturday, March 23, 2019 at Guam Veterans Chapel in Piti beginning at 9:00 am. Responso will be held at 11:00 am. And Burial with full military Air Force honors will follow. Condolences may be sent to his wife and family, Julie San Nicholas Iriarete Morris at 126 West Cueto Ave. Dededo, Gu 96929.

> From the Oval Office of the White House of
> the United States of America:
>
> *The United States of America
> honors the memory of
> Edward Allen Morris*
> *This certificate is awarded by a grateful nation in recognition of devoted and selfless consideration to the service of our country in the Armed Forces of the United States.*
>
> *Donald J Trump*
> *President of the United States.*

If that doesn't give you a moment to pause, kindly close the door as you leave our country.

Following are the twenty letters and emails that Ed's friends and family submitted for this book, in Ed's memory. Most, but not certainly all of Ed's friends were fellow YouTubers and chat room buddies. I have not edited or restructured any of these letters. Many of these letters are signed with their YouTube names, others have used their actual names. My role is now that of a reporter and not a writer. I am simply just an honored witness.

REMEMBERING OUR FRIEND ED

FROM: Julie Morris: aka Jules
Ed's wife of forty years.

When I first met my husband Ed, it was in Guam in 1978 at a bridal shower. When I first saw him from a distance, I told myself that I am going to be married to him. That day he asked me for a date, I turned him down. He asked me more than once, but that guy never gave up, lol. He asked me again and I finally went out with him. Ed was a gentleman, he opened the doors for me and he was my first love and the only one. We have three beautiful kids together. Our first child was born in Guam, we left Guam in 1979 and were stationed in California for two years then back to Guam where we had our second child, James Edward. We left Guam in 1985 and our youngest girl was born at Scott Air Force Base. We stayed there until Ed retired in 1995. Ed was in the Air Force for twenty-two years. He then worked for the railroad. This is hard to write down, we were together for forty years. We did a lot of fun things together, we went out to dinner even though having three kids we still managed to date. Then he got to know Eric and Christine (on-line) and everyone in the group was like a family. We had a good time and we love them all very much.

Ed was born in Japan, he's is Japanese and American. As you can see our kids take after their dad. Our son James takes after me, Oh boy! I miss him so much, he was the only guy I had for all of those years and I loved him.

    I know it will take time to heal but Ed will always have a place in my heart. David you are a sweet and a good friend, thank you so much from the bottom of my heart. Ed loves you all!

FROM: AnnaMarie Halverson (Morris): Ed and Jules eldest daughter

Hello Mr. Brown,
Sorry I'm just getting back to you. I have a really busy schedule with work and a baby so sometimes it takes up a lot of my time. I was able to answer your questions. Please let me know what you think. I was really close to my father Ed. I could go on and on. It has really been awhile since I've written an essay or something based on my life so please excuse my grammar.

There are so many good memories I have of times I spent with my dad. Seeing Dad in his Air Force uniform and how proud he was to serve his country. There was a time dad worked for Air Mobility Command at St. Louis airport and I used to go with him. He was such a hard worker and a good NCO, he took care of the soldiers and took care of the people flying with the military flights. Taking road trips to visit grandma and grandpa Morris in Knoxville, TN. Going to baseball games in St. Louis to watch those Cards play (our favorite) team. Our favorite football team is the 49ers. Ever since I could say my first words Dad and I used to always say during football season, "There ain't nothing finer than a 49er!" It probably sounds cheesy to others but it was our thing.

I remember Dad attending every one of my volleyball games and making sure that I always had my gear. I remember those nights that all dad wanted was for one of his kiddos to sit and watch those black-

and-white World War II movies on the History Channel. I usually was the last one standing and the other two went off to bed, they would be so bored and tired. But one of the most memorable would always be celebrating the big holidays at Dad and Mom's house, the smell and taste of all the wonderful food that Dad would put together and just the whole family being together spending every last second with each other. Dad was a good family man. He made sure his family always had what they needed even if he really did not have much money he always provided. He always told me how much he loved me, how proud of me he was. His last words to me before he passed was, "Anna, travel the world like you always wanted to, stay healthy, don't get cancer and I love you so much."

A life lesson Dad gave me was, "You can accomplish anything if you really put your heart to it." He also installed how family is important and that we should always be there for one another. These are things that I have taught my children and they have all taken these lessons with them and it has helped mold them into the individuals they are today.

Mr. Brown, thank you so much for writing this book and my Mother tells me that the proceeds will go to a charity. My father Ed would have loved this.

AnnaMarie Halverson (Morris)

FROM: James Morris
Ed's Son

I remember the first time dad and I went fishing at Silver Lake, it was a great time. Going to the Cardinals games and meeting Lou Brock. Going shooting with dad, and having fun with him, I miss him a lot.

James Morris

FROM: Christine Bomey
Ed's friend, Eric's Wife aka MZ.Bomey Zone

Here is my story. Thanks for making me cry again!

Where to begin, I guess at the beginning. I am writing about my dear friend Ed. I met him through Eric, who is my husband. Eric and Ed met through YouTube. There are quite a few of us in the YouTube group or community that came to know Ed.

Some, like myself, had a chance to meet him and his wife Julie who I call Jules and so did Ed. That was the beginning of our friendship, at least for me. I can remember that I would always pop in on a chat and say, hi. I would always ask, "Hey Ed, what are you drinking? He would almost always reply, "Two Hearted Ale." He loved that beer. Sometimes I would hang around and chat with him for a while, sometimes just to say hi.

I can never recall seeing him in a bad mood. Ed was never short with me or anyone else for that matter. He would always take the time to talk to you. Ed is one of the very few people that I considered a genuine person. He was the type when he asked, "How are you doing?" He really did care how you were. So that is how we met and became friends.

Now I would like to tell you my story of a very memorable moment. It was over five years ago. I had mentioned to Eric that I want a 44 magnum Smith and Wesson 629 classic, like in the 'Dirty Harry' movies.

So, Eric had mentioned that to Ed and said he would like to find one for my birthday. Keep in mind that at that time I had no idea of what was going on. I must mention that I am not one who likes surprises very much. That being said, let me continue, so the hunt was on for the handgun. Ed took it upon himself to find one for me and by the time it was my birthday. He looked for quite a while and passed on a few guns telling Eric that they weren't good enough for me. He definitely was on a mission. He finally found one! I remember that day. He had told Eric to videotape my reaction so he could see it as he could not be here in person. Of course, Eric did record that. He was sneaky about it for sure. So here is what happened.

    I came home from work that day which was my birthday and I believe that Eric, myself and family, were going to dinner but before that was going to happen Eric said he wanted me to watch Ed's video that he just put out there on YouTube which Ed recorded just for me. Eric said, "You've got to see the gun that Ed just purchased." So now I am watching the video and Ed has gotten the handgun that I so very much wanted. I was a bit disappointed but at the same time I was happy for him too. So Ed goes on to explain all about the gun and Eric is recording my reactions to all of this. Yes, I still did not have a clue as to what was going on. So by this time the video is almost done and for some reason Ed said he had to step away for a moment because he just noticed he did not have the paperwork he needed to register his new gun. I thought that was odd to do in a video. He comes back with the paperwork and looks at it as he said, "Wait a minute, this is not my gun! My name is not on here! This gun does not belong to me, it belongs to you Christine!" I looked at Eric and said, "What in the hell is going on?"

Eric came to the desk where I was watching the video and handed me a pistol case and in that case was the identical gun that I wanted. It was from Ed and Eric. Yes I was incredibly surprised. I never had anyone do something like that for me before. I kept on asking Eric if this was for real. At that point he told me he was recording all of this so he could send it to Ed. I've never met anyone that was so kind and thoughtful as Ed. We did a quick Google chat with him so I could say thank you. I told him that it was too much! He said no, and that he was very happy to do it for me, he smiled. We chatted for a few minutes and then we had to go, as we were meeting people for dinner.

The only thing that makes me sad, is when looking back on all of this, is that there was a time where we both had the same handgun and he was going to come to Minnesota for a visit and we were going to go shoot our matching 44 magnums together. That of course never happened. You know that saying….how does it go? "When they made Ed, they broke the mold." There will never be another one like him. In this case I do believe that is absolutely true. We should all be like Ed. Take time to help, support and care about one another. To this day I still have the gun and it will forever stay in my collection. I am truly blessed to be able to call Ed my friend.

Christine Richie-Bomey

#BeLikeEd

FROM: Eric Bomey: aka BandEBrewReviews aka Locked and Loaded

So David asked me for my story about Ed, well I am very lucky because I got to spend a lot of time with Ed. One of the first things Ed did for me was to send me his Ruger SR1911 commander. I had #BeLikeEd and EdUSAF laser engraved on it and I proudly carry it to this very day. One of the things that meant the most to me about Ed was if I was having a bad day I would either call Ed or jump on a video chat with him and in a matter of minutes he was able to make me feel better by his finding the good in every situation. I could go on and on with the times Ed was here.

It was day one of our, "Shootapolooza" get together's and we were all out in the backyard with the fire pit roaring and the grill cooking. Ed comes out to the back yard carrying a cheap domestic beer and walks up to me with this big smile on his face and I looked at the beer in his hand and slapped it out of his hand. The beer hit the ground and sprayed everywhere. I looked up at Ed and he didn't say a thing, he just looked at me with this look like somebody spanked his puppy. Without missing a beat, I reached down and opened the cooler and handed Ed a good beer as I said, "There little buddy." He got this look on his face like a young kid on Christmas morning and turned and walked away to go sit with the others at the fire pit. I think about it every day and miss him so very much. Love you Ed and I will see you again someday. #BeLikeEd

Eric Bomey
aka BandEBrewReviews aka Locked and Loaded

FROM: Lily Eller
aka Eric Bomey's eldest daughter

Ed always made my heart happy. No matter what, he had a smile for me and made me feel like I mattered. Every single time I joined a video chat he made a point of shouting out a cheery hello to me, even if that meant he had to interrupt someone. One stand-out memory was Ed's reaction to my art and his giggles over my bean doodles. He was one of the most genuinely kind people I've ever met in my life. I love Ed and will always value the time I got with him.

Lily Eller

**FROM: Black Widow Blanks:
aka John Solar, aka John Steinman**

David thanks for letting me have a part of this awesome piece of history.
So let's talk about my friend Ed Morris (EdUSAF)
Friend is the word that now has a different meaning. IN the past you could say friend and it needed some context. They may be your neighbor's, school pals, or using any number of ways to describe someone as to how you became friends.
But a new way has come to light in the past 15 years or so.
You now have a friend who means the world to you.
A friend you would do just about anything for.
Someone you've known for 10 years or more.
This friendship has a quite special trait, the fact that we have never met.
Countless video chats and YouTube talks with many emails, is how we talked.
This is the place where I met my friend Ed and what a friend Ed was!
Ed had time for everyone which is not an easy task but he made it seem effortless.
That seems like just kind words until people you have never heard of say, "Oh Ed USAF" and they tell you a story you have been hearing nonstop, "Yep he was so nice always commenting on my YouTube videos!"
And with no more than 24 hours in a day how did this man show love, kindness, and respect to so many?

Well I would have to say because my friend Ed Morris, WAS love, kindness, and respect to everyone. No matter how many, Ed always found room for you. Miss you buddy.

Black Widow Blanks aka John Solar aka John Steinman

FROM: Robert Christy

Ed always answered comments with a kind word. #BeLikeEd

Robert Christy

FROM: Bobby Paradise

I will miss the times Ed would call me late, after our chats. He would just tell me about his day. I do not know how, but Ed and I could be on the phone for hours. When my AR was not working right Ed (without asking me) sent me a set of KNS pins. Ed was a true blessing to me. I think about him all the time. I find peace in knowing I will see him in Heaven. Love you Ed. God bless brother.

Bobby Paradise

**FROM: Matt Wood
aka "TheRealCobraBurnout"**

      To be honest, I've been hesitant in attempting to put into words my memories of Ed. Nothing I write will hold a candle to the man Ed was. The words on paper, electronic or otherwise, don't stand a chance at holding the gravity of his soul. There is something to be said for a man that can grip the hearts of others through this crazy world of YouTube and Social Media. Ed was one of those for me. I never had the privilege of meeting him in the flesh. I knew him mainly from interactions on YouTube and Google Hangouts. EdUSAF was his YouTube channel name. When I saw that, I knew two things. One, I like this guy! Two, my YouTube channel name could have been way better then what I picked. Anyway, we did spend some time, face to face through the warm glow of computer screens, sharing Air Force stores amongst other things. He was, after all, my Air Force brother from another mother. Others would probably find most of what we shared, reminiscing about the Air Force to be a bit dull. But we got a chuckle out of it. And yes we did talk about muzzle brakes of all things. But like I mentioned before, YouTube was where I first met and interacted with Ed. Sadly Ed's last video on YouTube was a video response (VR) to me. Of all the things he could have made for his last video that was it…. water seems to accumulate in my eye region when I go watch it. It's a reminder that life is short, no matter your age, it's never enough.

Ed, you are truly missed! Thank you for sharing a part of your life with me. Ed, you helped me through some dark times brother. I'm still working on some things but you set the example for me to follow.

Thank you my friend, save me a seat in Heaven.
I love you Ed!

Matt Wood (aka TheRealCobraBurnout)
#BeLikeEd

FROM: Fabrizio Vianello
aka "Eltenda"

Ed and I were friends for a few years on YouTube and thanks to the "Shootapalooza" we were able to finally meet in person. I always felt that we knew each other for a long time. Ed had always been nice to me and really supportive of my American citizenship process. He was a true American, an awesome husband and a great father and a true friend that we are all going to miss.

Rest in peace our brother.
Fabrizio Vianello   aka Eltenda

FROM: SmileMoney
of Philadelphia PA

    My first individual memory with EdUSAF was four years ago when I commented on his videos of SINK-A-SHIP targets. Then out of the blue he sent me a package with several of them. I quickly went to the range and did a shootout video that I sent to him and had a great time playing this shooting game

    I forwarded a copy of the targets to another YouTuber to try to keep it going. Like so many gun channels, showing targets is a phobia, because they may blow the image they have developed. LOL!

    You will not find many of Ed's videos that I did not watch and comment on. We also had many private messages that we sent back-and-forth when that was a thing. We had several things in common, not only age. We even shared the same first name which I never use on YouTube because it belongs to him.

With deep respect
SmileMoney

FROM: Silverbk

I knew Ed. We spoke a bunch of times on the Google hangouts. I then met him in person at Eric's a couple of times and at, 'Shootapalazza' in Missouri. He was certainly in awe when we met all his YouTube friends in person at Eric's.

Ed was Japanese, he was adopted by an American serviceman. His father was also in the Air Force. Ed had a rivalry with him, and stayed in long enough to outrank him. After his father died the rivalry was over and Ed retired out of the Military.

He always wanted to help people. When he heard that my wife was selling nutritional supplements he bought some to support her. He then stopped taking them, his excuse was, his doctor took him off the supplements but I wonder if the wellness regime would have helped him.

You might think about that also. The nicotine and caffeine are going to catch up with you.

I have an Ed gun in my collection. It's a M1A rifle, new condition when I got it. Ed sold it to me to buy something else. For me, that particular Ed weapon will always remain with me. I tried my best to help Jules adjust to a life without Ed and offered to pay her 'blue book value' on Ed's entire gun collection to help her out financially. For some very sad reasons that didn't work out. Ed was a great guy. I miss him dearly.

Godspeed my friend.
Silverbk

FROM: Brad Thomas

So for Ed. My stories of Ed are always of him loving the pictures that I sent to the deplorables, especially Allison. I loved his videos with the women, he would use some of mine. When I went to Germany he asked me to get him the same shot glass as I've got, so I sent him one, he was happy as hell about it. The shot glass was from Dusseldorf. Every time I see the shot glass on my desk I think about Ed. He was always friendly on messenger and wanted to be a part of the gang. Everyone that knew or talked to Ed has the same consistent story that he was a great guy and would be very hard to dislike.

Brad Thomas

FROM: Jason Garrett
aka 'TheMultiGunman'
(Jason had hand written this note for Ed's memory book.)

The best memories I have of Ed are the interactions I had with him in the comment sections of various videos. He was a warm hearted and kind person. Ed never had a bad word to say about anyone. He would have given you the shirt off his back if you needed it. He was a representation of everything a decent human being should be.

Jason Garrett aka 'TheMultyGunMan'.

FROM: Kevin Ashbaugh
aka "EMTRailfan"

    Like many others in this awesome YouTube family, I was never fortunate enough to have personally met Ed or spoke with him outside of messages and comments, but he was someone who you felt like you had known for years from day one. We subscribed to each other through Eric Bomeys "BandEbrew reviews channels and Ed actually contacted me being a "railfan" and Ed being a railroader. Ed answered every single comment on this channel and commented on your videos quite often. He was a huge block in the foundation within this family. When it came to all the fundraisers that this family does for organization's or for each other in our times of needing help. Whether Ed was on the front lines or silently in the background, he was still spiritually helping.

    Everyone on this earth should, #BeLikeEd just a little, and it would make a big difference in our society.

We miss you Ed.

Kevin Ashbaugh aka "EMTRailfan"

#BeLikeEd

FROM: Jeremy Colson
aka "predawndeath"

My Duluth experience...
I will start by saying that it's hard to believe that I could meet so many like-minded assholes in one place. To tell my mom that I was going to Duluth and meeting up with people that I've never met and only know them from the Internet was an interesting start of the trip. What I expected and what I got were definitely two different things.

I expected to meet twenty random strangers that I couldn't possibly have anything in common with. Instead, I found lifetime friendships. It has always fascinated me that all these guys and girls from different parts of the country could come together because of YouTube and just instantly click.

When I met Ed and his wife Jules for the first time in person, it was like we already had been there....already had developed a bond but just never shook hands. I felt this bond with everyone I met. I was welcomed with open arms. It sure put my mind at ease and after a 4 1/2 hour drive. I was slightly nervous driving to a place where I've never been before, meeting a bunch of heavily armed patriots that I had never met and yet being greeted with handshakes, hugs and smiles. After days of shooting and evenings of drinking some of the finest craft beers with awesome people, I felt sad about leaving.

One week after I got home, Ed and Jules had sent me a surprise 'care package' with all of his favorite beers enclosed. The note read, "Have fun and enjoy with friends!" So that's exactly what I did. It's crazy how much of a family aspect there is with this group of guys and girls. It all started with, "Just some people I met on the Internet," has now evolved into, "People that I would fight and die for…..do anything for."

Jeremy Coulson aka "predawndeath"

FROM: Katlyn aka "PREDAWN POKEMON"

I had fun shooting and hanging out and meeting all of these new people, even though I wasn't very social to anyone because there were a lot of people. I got to do things I've never done before, go places that I've never been to and Duluth is a beautiful place to go and sight see. Loved hanging out with Mr. and Mrs. EBomey, Jeremy and Jules and of course can't forget David Brown, he is funny and I'm glad to have met him as well. I loved going to the falls and going to Spirit Mountain to ride the coaster and also love going to the Enger Park Tower. I also love going to the Aerial Lift Bridge and watching the big ships go through. I am glad Jeremy has taken me to Duluth and I hope that we can come back up again. Thank you all for making all of these gatherings possible.

Katlyn aka "PREDAWN POKEMON"

FROM: Glenn
aka "Agent Chaos"

    I first met Ed through YouTube, I had a prepping YouTube channel and Ed used to make comments on my videos occasionally.
  Then I switched channels and created the 'Agent Chaos' channel and Ed followed me there, then he found me on Facebook. Ed would leave comments on every single one of my videos and made comments on a lot of my posts on Facebook. I wasn't used to somebody like Ed. I originally thought that I had a stalker, but little did I know that he was just a genuine, friendly and caring person. Most of my communication with Ed was over the Internet. Unfortunately I only got to see him in person a few times, those few times I did. Ed treated me as if we had been best friends for our entire lives. He was just a really good dude. He was the kind of guy that if he considered you a friend you are a part of his family. I believe that Ed would do anything he possibly could for a friend, he gives me faith that people can be good. It's rare to meet someone who is just generally a friendly person like he was. The only regret I ever will have about meeting Ed is that our time together was so short.

Glenn aka "Agent Chaos"

FROM: Matt Grau aka "Jarlaxle85"

I never had the opportunity to meet Ed but because of Ed and a great group of people, I've heard a good amount of stories. If Ed was anything like the group of people I have met I know I'd be saying he was a dang good man, because this group of people will help any of the others when needed. This group I speak of is a heck of a group. We have had lots of fun and many stories. Most of all, I call them family and one, I am proud to be a part of.

Matt Grau aka "Jarlaxle85"

FROM: Poco Loco

Every morning I would wake up to a short message or just a Hello from Ed. He did a lot of webcam chats. He would be the first to greet people when they came into the chats. I honestly think he loved life. He always had a smile even when he had pain.

Poco Loco

FROM: Battle Bean

I used to give Ed a shot by telling him, "Most of the stuff you worked on in the military are museum pieces today." The song by Adele, "Hello" reminds me of Ed.

Battle Bean

FROM: Ray Edwards

These are some of the final texts I shared with Ed.

Me: Hey bro just checking on you how are you feeling, what is the prognosis for recovery from this cancer?

Ed: Hi brother I am well and being treated with chemo once a week and radiation daily for 6 weeks prognosis is good. Good to hear from you.

Me: Awesome that's great news man I'll be praying for you over here and yes good to hear from you. I have been trying to create those memories with the kiddos as much as I can. Anyway, I'll keep in touch.

Ed: Ya man I'll try as well, that's great keep it up build as many memories as you can.

Me: Yes sir!

The last time I saw Ed was at the hospital just before he passed. He was unconscious and I hope he heard me. I prayed for him with his family by his bedside. I told him I loved him.

I miss my friend

Ray Edwards

#BeLikeEd

FROM: Travis Eller

Hey buddy, Eric told me I needed to try to get this over to you tonight so here it is below. Feel free to fix any grammar or spelling issues because let's face it, I went to public school.

Ed was one of the most honest and true people that I have ever had the privilege of meeting in my life. Unfortunately I did not have long to share a friendship with Ed. As is the case with many of us, I met Ed through our group of friends through our video chats along with our YouTube videos and interactions. As I came to know him and learned his story and met him and his family, I came to realize that this was someone special and the type of person you don't meet every day. Ed was selfless and generous. He just had this way about him that could bring a glow to any room and always made you laugh. Unfortunately we lost our friend too early as we do with many of the best people we will ever meet. This friend, this Patriot, is a true American who will be missed everyday by those who will remember and love him for the rest of our lives. Every time I look at my Mosin rifle that came to me through Ed, I close my eyes and remember our short time together. All of the laughter, the fun, the beers, the late nights and the fellowship through our discussions and interactions. I love my friend Ed and I miss my friend. Ed's memory we'll live on forever.

Travis Eller

CHAPTER 8 So... Why aren't we?

Our shared and common battle cry is, "#BeLikeEd" (thank you Gunwild) but the question begs to be asked, why aren't we already, like Ed? This question brings me back to the definitions of who Ed is, not was, but is. Ed still lives because we carry him in our hearts, so therefore Ed is and not was. Sitting here now and looking at these twenty-one pages of Ed's friends comments, along with the stacks and stacks of research papers with my proofread discarded writings will tell all that Ed had game. My word count currently stands at 91 book pages (the standard novel size of 6x9 inches) 24,118 words, in my attempt to describe this group and in describing who Ed is. For me, I can reduce it all down to just one word in describing who Ed is. My one word (perhaps just my one word) is simply, "Reacher." Ed is a reacher, he reaches out to people, he spends numerous hours corresponding with people because he knows that at some point we all need validation. Validation is a rare and frightening gift to receive. Few of us know what to do with it. It's like a foreign body or maybe like some of shit Eric eats that he gets in the mail from China.

I would be remiss if I didn't take you for a stroll through my many writings. I know that few of our members have bothered to read my other four novels and that's OK. You are amongst the majority. My drive in my writing has nothing to do with wealth or fame, because I have great evidence of neither. I, much like many others at times, feel like I'm the Capuchin monkey with the tin cup on the organ grinder's shoulder. I want people to tell me how cute I am and I do little tricks to amuse you, so you will like me even more. But if you try to reach out to touch me, I will see that as a threat to myself and my organ grinder and I will attack. I will attack, not like a monkey but like a fucking gorilla! Oftentimes the reason I attack is for fear that your touch will cause me to want more. At some point I know that your touch will go away and I will be left all alone again. If I don't allow you to touch me, then you can't hurt me.

  All four of my novels carry the same theme throughout and that theme is how we can win over fear and transfer to faith. Fear is not a word, fear is an acronym and that acronym stands for:

  False--Evidence--Appearing--Real

  Why don't I tell you who I am? Because if I do, I'm afraid that you may not like me! So we all do the acceptance dance and we smile, we smile when we don't feel like smiling, we laugh when we're not happy, we emotionally dress to the occasion. That occasion being, I'm okay (but I'm lying). As most all people, we protect our emotional vulnerabilities at all costs, even more than we protect our own lives at times. Did Ed have fear? Of course he had to have fear. How did he circumvent that fear? He didn't embrace it, he embraced hope and that was hope for all.

Does anyone remember the fellow that almost did well? Of course not, nobody remembers someone who almost did or who almost tried.

To be remembered we have to become memorable and that is in short is how we can be like Ed, be memorable.

Chapter 9 A STAR IS BORN

This is my final chapter in this book. I will now be turning the writing over to my dear friend Christine. It's all on her now, at the end of this chapter to the end of the book is all her. I will not edit or suggest anything within her work.

I can tell you all that working with Christine is like taking a bus full of preschoolers to the, "Build A Bear" Store. Speaking of buses, John Solar constantly ribs Christine about her driving the wheels off the bus. Well John, I think I need to correct you in that area. Christine has no business driving a bus, maybe a small Van with training wheels but certainly not a bus. Not ever a bus! This idea of inviting Christine in as a co-author in this work came to me upon awakening just a few days ago.

I of course, like many others, wonder how in the hell could a man write about someone who he has never even met. I answered myself with; how many people write about astronomy who've never been to the dark places in the Galaxy? For me this came quite easily. Looking into the eyes of Eric, Christine and of course Jules, tells me all that I need to know about Ed. The twenty-one people that contributed to this book have further told me of Ed in much greater detail. So I used Christine to be my guiding light and she damn near blinded me!

I think it would be fitting to start at the beginning of our friendship. I do have to say that I somewhat miss the early days of us getting to know each other. Christine in times past, would look at me as just another friend of Eric's that's probably a total poopy-head.

You know how it is when you first meet someone, how you try to act interested and look at them, but you're thinking that you would rather fold the clothes in the dryer?

Sadly that didn't last very long with Christine. Christine has a unique way of leaning forward and looking at me from different angles. I'm sure she is asking herself, "What in the hell is he saying now, I know damn well that he is setting me up for something again!"

As I have stated in my other books, "I write to stir the soul, not with a wooden mixing spoon but with a Canoe paddle." This joint venture is much the same with an even larger Canoe paddle, much larger!

This is the very first text I sent to Christine while she was at work. I love to catch her off guard where she can't openly respond and call me bad names, it's a fun game and I don't think she likes playing it. Here are the texts we've shared from the beginning of this venture. She's gonna kill me for this!

Friday May 14th 9:44 AM 2021
    Me: You ready to get large and have your name on the cover of a book as a co- author?

Christine: Ummm Ok.... now what are you talking about?

Friday 10:00 AM

Me: (I sent her a picture of page one with her name as a co-author and the new title, "#BeLikeEd" with the subtitle of, "Celebrating a Life Well Lived."

I told her, "The last half of the book you become a legitimate co-author. You tell our readers about your journey, your mental, emotional, and spiritual experience for the times we have spent together and how you have been affected by the loss of Ed. I want the pros and cons of a greater understanding of yourself and others. Are you in?

I will not feed you your questions or your observations. This will be all you. It's going to be like we live on opposite ends of the earth. You have the unique ability to define emotions and behaviors that I don't have.

Christine: Wow! I'm truly flattered that you would choose me to be a part of this journey... I am at a loss for words which don't happen very much, Lol. So can I call you after work and we can discuss this a bit more? Would that be OK?

Me: Sure babe, you can speak of the value of understanding and overlooking people's weaknesses while still supporting them in your friendships. You do that shit all the time. People can and need to learn from you. Hell you do it on your Podcast every week. Give me a call when you get home from work. It will be a simple Podcast in print.

Christine: Will do.

Friday 7:23 PM
     Me: How you doing on your writing? Bunkie is thrilled about your writing. She, as I do, believe in you.
Friday 7:36 PM
     Christine: Trying to put my thoughts together. I have 334 words so far.
     Me: Champion! That equals one whole page of the 6 x 9 book.
     Christine: Oh 1 page....??? I truly appreciate your writing.

Saturday 4:53 AM
     Christine: Been up since 3:30 this morning and I am up to 909 words so far.
Saturday 7:20 AM
     Me: Hate me yet, or should I say, do you hate me even more worser?
     Christine: Nope.....It's not an easy process.
     Me: Easy peasy. Let your heart be your guide. Trust you, be you.
Saturday: 8:07 AM
     Me: I think we need some ground rules. 1st, this is not a race. Next you can't allow this to own you. This is not a summer project. Relax, be you and tell your story just like we talk at any other time.
     I'm still the boss of you and I will allow you to call me several bad names each day. Your name will be in the same size font as mine on the cover.
Saturday 8:32 AM

#BeLikeEd

    Christine: I know it's not a race but when the thoughts start swarming in my head that is when I like to write. Much like how I do my podcast and journals. Don't worry, if I have questions or issues I will come kicking on your door. Just sayn.
    Me: Yah sweet thang you.

    During all these back-and-forth texts, we also had several phone calls back and forth as well. I told Christine that she needed to take a picture of herself, she of course wanted to know why. I told her it was not her business, just like her Nonna used to tell her and John's Nonna (on loan) told him. "Mind your business, that's his business, mind yours!"
    I wouldn't characterize myself as an impatient fellow. I'm more like an unreasonably demanding SOB and I want that shit now! Christine sent me two side-by-side photographs.

Sunday 4:11 PM
    Christine: You choose, I like them both.
    Me: Gotta be the first one, it says, "Are you sure you want to talk to me like this?"
    Christine: Okay
Sunday 4:46 PM
    Me: Gonna use it for the back cover.
    Christine: I thought so...this is quite the journey!
    Me: You've always been for reals, now you get to be even more realsier.

I posted that picture on Facebook and I was giving Christine the running counts on the people who liked her photograph.
Sunday: 7:27 PM
    Me: 59 people so far, thank you are the bee's knees and the post has only been up for 47 minutes!
    Christine: That truly is amazing.
    Me: I am proud of you.
    Christine: Thank you.
Monday 8:12 AM
    Me: 77 people think you're groovy!
    Christine: Ooohhh the numbers are growing. I shared it with my family in Canada too!
    Me: Good girl.
Monday 3:32 PM
    Me: Still love me Babe?
    Christine: Writing away.
    Me: Me too.
    Christine: I am curious to see what our friends think after they read this.
Monday 7:14 PM
    Me: They will love it and tell you, or they may think you could have done a better job. Well either way, you did what you did to the very best of your ability. There will always be people who want to think they could have done a better job but they were not selected, you were. This is our work and we own it and we will apologize to no one. Keep your focus, this is for Jules and maybe just a bit for you and Eric and John. It's about healing, not pleasing. Write your story your way.

I was laughing as we were talking about this over the phone. I was laughing about other people's expectations or their thinking that I somehow need their approval.

I sent her two emails that I received just this morning, within four minutes of each other. I told her this was just a very small sample of where the 'Fame Train' is going to be derailed. One is from a Facebook friend who asked me to help her write her book. I played the twenty question game with her (which is a weekly game I get to play with aspiring writers) who probably will never step near an ink pen.

Me: What is your book about?
Her: I haven't decided.
Me: Why do you want to write a book?
Her: I'm not sure.
Me: Do you hope to gain favor within your family or of a romantic interest?
Her: I don't think so.
Me: Have you read my four novels?
Her: No, I just want to be famous. I just want to be called an Author.
Then it finally came, "Do you think you could help me with it if I told you all about me, but it's almost like a secret?"
Me: I am sorry, but I am a full time, 12 hour plus a-day novelist. I just don't have the time.
She said thanks and it was finally over.

I have had to develop a system for leaving those people with their dignity and yet not allowing them to steal my time away from me. I just simply tell them that I charge a dollar a word. The lowest word count for a novel is 80,000 words, so that equals $80,000 which is payable in full, before I began to write one sentence. That seems to help them find a different or better way perhaps. That is right after they inform me that I'm a greedy selfish bastard, most often times.

Tuesday 7:10 AM
    Christine: Lmao...is this what I have to look forward to?
    Me: You bet your ass you do.
    Christine: Guess that I'll be practicing the word NO a lot.
    Me: Remember those emails were just 4 minutes apart. Welcome to the fame train! Hell of a topic for one of your shows.
    Christine: Yes, I think not only do a show about the book but a separate one as well. Kinda like a behind the scenes thing to talk about that stuff. Shall I book you for two shows then?
    Me: Seven is a nice round number, that would make John Solar lose his shit, but two shows will be just swell.
    I sent Christine a copy of the new cover with her name on it. She responds, "OK, you're funny." I guess I spelled her maiden name wrong. I guess there's no 'T' in Richie. Well I took care of that then she comes back with, "ok thanks."
Tuesday 12:52 PM

Christine: Seeing my name on that page makes it really real now, just saying!

Me: That's the plan. Now you need to send that to your friends and family.

Tuesday 1:48 PM

Christine: Well I just burnt through my entire break, sending all of my friends a copy of my name on the first page. They are really excited and want to know how it all comes out.

Me: Then you better get busy.

Christine: I will get it done.

Wednesday 7:54 AM

Me: How in God's name do you spell nanoon? You know, the name you and John used for your grammas. Spell it please?

Christine: Nonna. What are you up to now?

Me: Not your business.

Christine: OK sniper.

Me: Two clicks to the left.

Christine: On target.

Me: Love you Babe. John tells me that his Nonna oftentimes would say, "Mind your business," with a wooden spoon in her hand, it made him wonder if she was going to stir something or swat his ass.

Christine: Most likely to swat yah if you got out of line.

Wed 11:18 AM

Me: I feel pretty, oh and P.S.my part is done.

Christine: Yeah. I'm halfway through mine which isn't bad since unlike some people I know.... I am not retired lol. Seriously, I can't wait to read it. I think we're going to knock this one right out of the park.

    Me: Two parks, I'm thinkin.

Wed 5:05 PM

    Christine: I hate you right now as I am writing. Just sayn.

    Me: You ain't the first.

    Christine: Nor am I the first that wants to kick you in the balls!

    Me: My entire ball's?

    Christine: I am done.... 7,507 words, 32 pages. The number 32 is one of my favorite numbers. I am going to sleep now. Mentally and emotionally exhausted. Talk soon.

    Me: Night brave girl.

8:21 AM

    Me: Still love me....kinda?

    Christine: Yeah I'm tired today.... took a while to wind down before sleep last night.

    Me: Yup, memories and emotions are a tough deal. Just keep in mind that joy and pride (not the Joey kind of pride) are our rewards!

    Christine: Had strange dreams too.... emotions have a way of getting into your subconscious. So I am going to read what I wrote one more time to make sure it all makes sense and that it has a flow too. I think for some it's going to really hit them in the feelers. Yes it does feel good to complete it.

    Me: Some say... some plan... and some do. You do and what you do best is doing you. And that

you... that you do is remarkable. Celebrate being the gift of you!
9:14 AM
    Christine: Ok so what comes next?
    Me: Hugs
10:18 AM
    Me: Now do this… listen to the Tears for Fears song, "Shout." Then download the lyrics. Keep those lyrics next to you when you get home and put on your jammies, sink into the couch with your headphones on and play it over several times. It will be the most cleansing emotional shower of all of your life. Trust me and do it.

    Now back to the book and more importantly back to Christine. I used every text I sent for a very specific reason. I kind of have to act like a coach or perhaps a parent. I have to convince Christine that she has the skills to do this. It's up to me to give her the support that she needs to believe that she can do this. It's like showing a small child how to catch a ball, you need to encourage them to do something that they don't believe that they can do. Then you show them that they can do it, and they will do it, all because you believed in them. Make no mistake, Christine has exemplary social skills and she carries a high level of success in communicating with people, especially with her podcasts.

    We all need a bit of a nudge and a bit of a nod of approval at times. Admittedly there have been times, many times actually, that I had my own doubts of my abilities as an author. I keep a number of letters from both readers and reader friends that I will go back to when I'm feeling lost or over my head. I received a very kind and supporting text from my pal Rod Hixson just two days ago. I was jokingly posting on Facebook that each of my four novels sells for half the price that a box of ammunition does. I also added my web address to that post. It's my sneaky way to advertise my books and website on Facebook for free. I have paid a lot of money for Facebook ads in the past with lousy results.

So now back to the Rodney Hixson story. He wrote in response to my joke: "That's because what's on the inside of your books is priceless.

On a random thought sounds like a sales opportunity, buy a book, get a Box of ammo! New book price is $59.99 (depending upon caliber)!

Hope you are doing well my friend. I'm very happy to see where this all is taken you. I'm proud of you for the chances that you have taken, especially when the odds were against you. A wise, great man once told me, "Dare to dream!" I'm just happy to see that man living up to his own advice!"

Well that itself is a beautiful notation that makes the tallest of mountains look climbable. But there's a back story to this that I think you'll find even more interesting.

I worked for a security company that contracted their services with Rodney's employer. It was made clear to me by my supervisor during my training that my predecessor was a do nothing, slacker and was not at all respected or desired at Rodney's employer's location. After a week's training with the 'slacker' I went solo.

On my third day of that assignment I met Rod Hixson, and it didn't go well. As I entered the building Rod came down the stairs two at a time with fire in his eyes as he said, (like a pissed off daddy) "You need to calm down!" I assumed he was talking in reference to a minor confrontation I had with one of the contract drivers for the company. I looked up at Rod (who was still three steps above me and he stands over six feet tall). I felt myself flexing and I wanted to just flat, lay him out! I explained to him in (a somewhat elevated and firm tone of voice) that I was doing exactly what Mike Schmidt (product loading supervisor) told me to do and the way he told me to do it."

I motioned to Rod with a head nod to follow me as I went into the operations office where Mike Schmidt works. (It was obvious to me that there was a long term standing tension between them. I'm thinking they were actually friends but the stress and demands of each of their jobs put them at odds.)

I told Mike Schmidt, 'Schmidty' (who I actually liked) that Rod was having trouble with the way I was doing things, the things that he told me to do. I told them both, "You guys work this shit out amongst you, I am not a part of this. Tell me what you want and that's what I will give you, but don't put me in the middle of your bullshit." As a footnote, Mike 'Schmidty' and Rod are dear friends to me and I visit with them each time I go back to Colorado.

And that my friends is how a lifelong friendship begins. I never thought I could be pals with a bunch of forklift slingers in a warehouse/shipping setting.

I have to say that from that job, I also had the pleasure of meeting some great guys, many of whom are still my friends today. My pal Dan Hare, was a lot of fun and a true gentleman. Part of Dan's job was to check in the truck drivers and seal the 'bonded' loads before they were released. I was the truck rustler and staged the trucks for loading. After Dan sealed the trucks he would come over to me and we would bullshit for a while. Dan treated the truck drivers (mostly owners/operators) with a great deal of respect. Warehouse workers aren't always known for their sensitivities towards people. But Dan was different, in that respect. Dan treated everyone like he was glad to see them, he could bring out a smile from the most hard bitten, road weary trucker who was more than a bit short on patience and social skills. Dan was an EMT/Firefighter back in his hometown in Wisconsin. I think Dan was the way he was because of his time in EMS and the fact that he and Rod and Schmidty were all raised right by their parents.

One of the other of the many letters I review on a regular basis when I'm feeling in doubt, comes from,

Lisa McElveen Ramsing. I have known Lisa as a Facebook friend for about six years or more. We check in with each other on a regular basis. Lisa was a medic and firefighter who is now retired. She lost her firefighter husband of thirty-one years (and her heart), while he was fighting a fire. Lisa knows of what she speaks and she knows of what I speak as well. In her texts Lisa addresses me as, "Sir David." Lisa recently wrote:

"Sir David, even through the heartaches you have had to endure along life's way from being that little boy that wanted to leave this world, I thank God and the Duluth Police Department that you didn't. Instead you truly became a wonderful giving, encouraging gentleman that you are today. God had a plan for you because through you, God gave all of us blessings through your writings by telling your story. While reading your books, I felt as if I was walking right next to you, seeing and feeling the heartaches and triumphs that life threw at you. As an old medic and firefighter, I thank you for telling your stories so well and showing us we are not alone. Love through Christ my dear friend. Always, Liz and Molly Rose."

Lisa has a cat named Molly Rose and Molly Rose also writes to me with the help of her mommy. Lisa is like a little sister to me, as a few other Facebook friends are. I won't let them pay for my books, as to me, they are family. I always mail Lisa's book first on the very day they arrive.

Well that pretty much does it for my end of this book and now I would like to introduce to you my dear friend and first time novelist, Christine Richie Bomey. It's all yours Babe.

I will leave you with this:
If you are someone to someone,
then you are somebody.

And this:
Dreams are worth Dreaming
Dare to Dream my friends
And
Dream BIG!

God Bless America

#BeLikeEd

MENDING MY BROKEN HEART

Hello, my name is Christine Richie-Bomey, and I can now say that I am a first-time published author. Still trying to digest that statement. This is my very first book! I am so thankful for my dear friend David Brown for allowing me to be a part of this book. He has been with me every step of the way on this journey. I must confess this is something I would never have dreamed or thought of doing, but here I am. For me this is stepping outside of my box. This opportunity presented itself and I took it. This journey has been many things but dull is not a word I would use to describe it. I would also like to take a moment to thank my husband Eric for all of his love and support too. I hope you enjoy reading this as much as I enjoyed writing it.

Did you ever have someone that passed away that you cared about and another person that didn't know him or her? "Can you tell me about him or her?" Well, that person would be Ed Morris. If I had to describe Ed using only one sentence it would be that he was a very gracious person. He is like no other friend and don't get me wrong, all my friends are unique in their very own way. Lately, I have thought more about Ed, especially in this past year. You see, Julie or Jules as I like to call her (and so did Ed), makes me see how much you should appreciate people in your life because as they say, "Life is short".

Unfortunately, this is not the first time that I have been up close and personal, watching as my friends have lost their husbands. Wendy was the first, she lost her husband Christopher who is another close friend of mine. I remember when Wendy had texted me that day because she was concerned that she had not heard from Christopher. It was October in northern Minnesota. He drove a Semi Truck. Winter some years, can come on fast in the North Country and this year it did. I told her not to worry, it probably was just something to do with the cellular towers not working correctly. She kept trying his phone and continuously got voicemail. She said to me she had an awful bad feeling about this. Some time had passed and the next thing I knew I'm receiving a call from her. She said law enforcement found her at work and they came to tell her about Christopher's accident. Just like that he was gone. I remember asking her if she wanted us to stop by after I was done with work, and she said yes. Eric and I went to her home. It was amazing to see how much support she got from family and friends. Let me tell you, it sucks bearing witness to all of it as a friend, because there isn't much that you can do about it but be there to support them. It's not like you have a magic wand or Genie to bring them back. I can say that I am blessed and grateful for the time that I got to spend with them both.

I keep in touch with Jules, we talk almost every day. She is in Illinois, and I am here in Northern Minnesota. Sometimes she tells me stories about Ed and how much she misses him. Rightfully so, as they were together for over 40 years.

    I enjoy her stories and I'm glad to listen, laugh, and cry with her. Ed was truly the love of her life, and she dearly misses him. You just never know how much time that you have with that spouse or family or friend. You never know if you will have that time to say all the things that you need or want to say. Sometimes the people we care about can leave us suddenly and we don't get a chance to say goodbye. Either way it sucks! I always remember the saying I saw from Harley-Davidson...the one on my coffee cup that reads, "It's not the destination it's the journey". Isn't that true about life?

    Ed was a person who I believed understood that. He never tried to take anything for granted. They say people come into our lives for a reason or a season. Ed's case, I think it was both. Our group's motto is, "#BeLikeEd" but how many of us put that into practice on a daily basis? Don't get me wrong, we all have our own trials and tribulations in life that are thrown at us, but it's how we react to those issues or situations that make the difference. I think Ed had a lot of those life experiences and that is how he became who he was. There are many qualities that I admire about him, but the one that stands out the most for me is how he didn't judge people. He took them as they are. I believe this is one lesson that is the hardest in life that people must learn.
There will always be something special in every

person that you meet who you don't like or agree with, but if you can get past that you could have a friendship or a relationship with that person, then I think you're on the right track. We as a people are so damn quick to judge or put labels on people that it's just absolutely ridiculous. We really need to stop doing this and just see the person. A perfect example of this is, when we would invite people, we met from the YouTube community who shared a common interest such as myself and Eric. They would come to our house on Labor Day weekend. It was what we called our "Shootapalooza". This was a fun and safe weekend with people getting together to shoot guns. The first time I got to meet Ed and Jules in person, was when they came for one of the "Shootapalooza's." I believe it was back in 2015. Prior to their coming to visit, there were a lot of Google chats, and texting between Eric and Ed. When we finally got to meet them and say hello, it was kind of like saying hi to an established old friend. We got to spend some time with Ed and Jules. I must say looking back at it, I wish that I would have had more time to visit not just with them but the rest of the people that came here throughout the years. Mind you, I was the only one doing the cooking, planning and cleaning and anything else that needed to get done. Yep, I can be a control freak about certain things, this being one of them. This was mostly Eric's time to hang with the boys and that's OK with me, because I get my time to hang with my girlfriends at my annual dinner party which is a lot of fun. I have great friends and have much love for them. Jules had the opportunity to experience one of these dinner parties a few years back.

Anyway, Jules and I hit it off and before you know it, she was right there helping with everything. So, here's where I need to pause and tell you of some of the behind the scenes activities. I am hoping that no one takes this out of context. This is my truth and observations that I have made through the years of hosting the annual "Shootaplooza's."

First, I want to ask if you can possibly understand how much work is involved in making this happen throughout numerous years? I am the maid, the cook, and the party planner. I put together the menu for the whole weekend. Not to mention if we decided to go out to dinner, I would need to suggest a restaurant too. It was just one of the many hats that I wear during this time, which starts long before everybody gets here. There were some years that I couldn't take any time off from work, and I just had my three-day weekend. People would come early like on a Wednesday or Thursday. So, I had to make sure that I got things organized and done long beforehand. Here is where I want to give a shout out to my good friend Mary, who has been helping me throughout the years of these events. She has given up a weekend or two each year to help me prepare the lasagna and anything else that we could get done ahead of time. I make my special sauce by scratch, which takes the entire day. I make it just like my nonna and my mom taught me. Let's not forget all the multiple food shopping excursions that must be done in order to make this all happen. Guests who have had my family's lasagna rave about it every year.

Most years Eric and I paid for the annual dinners. Here's where I have to say that some of our friends have pitched in every year to help with the cost of all the meals. So, a big thank you to you all! There's no need to do any shout outs, you know who you are. After spending the entire day making the specialty meat sauce (in the biggest pots I own) there is an assembly line of putting the lasagna together, which in years past, I have to say we had quite a line going. It would be Mary from Wisconsin, Jules from Illinois, Christie from Louisiana, and myself (from parts unknown), all in the kitchen. One thing that I will say is that spending time in the kitchen cooking with my friends is the best, it reminds me of the years gone by that I was able to cook with my nonna and my mom and have that greatly anticipated Sunday family dinner. Those were fun and special memories that I have of her and my mom.

When the four of us girls were cooking in the kitchen, we were like a well-oiled high-speed running piece of machinery. Most years went off without a hitch and we got better at making it. Some years Mary and I would make the Lasagna ahead of time and freeze them until it was time to bake them. Each year I got better at organizing it all. It was also a good time for the four of us girls to catch up while we were busy cooking and serving dinner. One year we had about forty people for dinner. That was nine pans of lasagna and let's not forget the salad and breadsticks. That's one hell of a meal, if I do say so myself. There were many hours of prep work with organizing it all to make sure that nothing was forgotten. I can't tell you how many lists I have made.

We also had people staying with us which meant we had to get the spare bedrooms ready. Each year the experience taught me better how to organize which was great, as it allowed me more free time and in that free time, I would grab a glass of wine and sit by the fire pit and try to relax. Often that just wasn't possible especially when you have a house full of people and alcohol is involved. I will get to that part in a minute. I must admit I was not very keen on the idea when Eric first brought all of this upon me.

Now boys and girls here's where men and women think differently. Eric, my hubby didn't see any issue with inviting people to our house to stay, eat, and hang out with us. I thought he was bat shit crazy! Invite people that we met on the Internet? Sure, I knew them, but I didn't really know them! He didn't think it was a big deal, but I did! Hell, I don't know these people and you want them to come and stay with us? Just open my home to all? I am not a bed and breakfast joint. We had many discussions with me shouting at him sometimes about this. Looking back, I'm glad that we did. That was a big leap to take. We had made friends from all over the United

States, Canada and Scotland. Most of the folks we kept in touch with and others not so much. You know how it is, people get busy, life gets in the way and so there's that. We also have gotten invites in the past to visit and stay with friends at their homes too.

That is one of the positives but I can't just talk about the positives without bringing up the negatives, well at least in my book. Let's go back to the previous statement that I made about a house full of people with alcohol involved. Some of you are my friends, who have been here and are now reading this. Please don't get mad at me. Try to see and understand it from my perspective. If you're not ready to read my truth, then feel free to skip ahead. Just saying. The funny thing about people and alcohol is that you just never know how they will act. I would be remiss if I didn't say here and now, that these wonderful people were extremely cautious and respectful when it came to handling firearms. All firearms were cleared, cased and put away before any alcohol came out.

Now back to guests and alcohol especially when they are a guest at my home. Let me tell you right here and now that I was raised, "Old school" and was taught to have respect and consideration for people and their homes. There is a whole list of what is acceptable and what is not, at least in my world. Now I can honestly say that everyone got along while drinking and no fights ever broke out, but that doesn't mean shit didn't happen because it did! Case in point, I learned a few years ago that my laundry sink in the basement, you know the old style that you would find in a farmhouse made from cement and is a good size one. This sink of mine was used as a damn urinal!

Those boys thought it was funny to, "Piss in the sink". However, I didn't find it funny, not at all. So, let me ask you this, if I were to be invited to your home and I decided not to use the bathroom, or the biff, would you think it OK for me to pee on your floor or in one of your sinks? Many jokes were made about it, and I decided not to get upset as it could cause a fight or scene. I didn't want the drama or to waste the time or energy. I think if I had shown how pissed off I really was, I think some would have been pissed off at me or would have been offended because they thought it was no big deal. So, you come to my home and do that, and I am supposed to be OK with it? Really? I know it isn't good to bring up things from the past and I need to learn to let it go, but you all were either, too drunk and acting stupid or maybe you were just too lazy to walk to the bathroom. Either way this was not OK with me. FYI....from this point forward this is not acceptable in my home. I don't appreciate it. OK, let's move on, shall we?

So now I will move onto another story I would like to share with you. There were many weekends when several of our friends would stay up all night. Eric would stay up with them too. It was either drinking or flapping their gums all night long. This time they were in the basement, where the "man cave" area is and just above them, on the ceiling is our smoke detector. Some of them were vaping and made the alarm go off at 5:30 am in the morning while the rest of us were still sleeping! I had someone sleeping on the couch in the living room and I tell you that person suddenly woke up and got up! That damn alarm is loud! Good morning! Yeah! I think not! I went flying down the stairs and by that time everyone was trying to scatter like mice. Gone! I got to the alarm and turned it off and now I'm standing there in my pajamas with a severe case of bed head. I looked a mess!

That was the least of my issues at the moment. However, I wanted to know who was smoking or vaping downstairs in my home to set off the smoke alarm. I was mad as hell and heads were about to roll! I was so mad with having to deal with this shit rather than being able to sleep-in. Come on! By the time I'm done cooking and cleaning, I'm dog assed tired. I just want to get a good night's sleep. Eric saw how mad I was, and he didn't say a word, which was damn smart on his part. Anyway, after I calmed down a bit, I gathered all who were involved and had a tempered conversation. There was one person that didn't think it was a big deal or so it seemed, which made me mad all over again! So, let me ask you how would you like it if I came to your home and did some shit like that especially when you had friends from out of town staying at your home? Just dismiss it as no big deal? They didn't think vaping was going to cause a problem. I had to have a, 'come to Jesus' moment with some of them to make them understand this is my home, and it was not cool with me. Everyone stayed out of my way for the rest of the day. I don't understand people sometimes, if you do shit and you don't own it, well that's like saying sorry not sorry. In that moment when you know you're in the wrong, own that shit. That's when you need to say, "My bad!" Otherwise, you make the person that you did or said that to, feel like you don't care about them, and they are of no value.   Acknowledgement and validation can go a long way with me and others. I am not saying it's easy and yes, it's something we all need to work on daily, myself included. My mom always said that, "Actions speak louder than words" and she was right. I learned that there is more than one side of the story, and that it should be taken into consideration as well. Take out of this what you will. I just wanted to be clear about how I felt and what I thought. As for me, I'm trying to let things go and not stay mad. Besides, that it will only feed the negative appetite that we all have inside of us that at times, doesn't need to grow. I do think if you pay attention, life is trying to give you a lesson whatever that may be, and you should try to learn from it. It just makes things better in the long run. I know change is hard blah blah blah. Here ends the sermon. Listen, this hasn't been easy for me to write about it.

    The only other person that gave me a push to step outside of the box is my dear friend John Solar. Together we do two podcasts, one is a Monday through Friday show and it's called, "A Quickie with Mz B." We are just two wing nuts having a lot of laughs and this podcast has no politics at all. The other podcast is, "Mz. Bomey Zone" and that one is done live every Saturday night (on Spreaker, iHeart and several other channels) at 8:00 pm Central time. That one has topics all over the place with lots of laughs. Ed listened to the shows all the time. The only shows he missed were when he worked weekends. I really do enjoy doing both shows with John. There was a time when I thought I would never understand this whole concept of the podcasts. John was and is still very patient with me. He is a good teacher too. He is a smart guy and can be a total smartass sometimes. I look at it this way, if he didn't like me, he wouldn't be picking on me. I have the same motto. Also, I have to say that John is one of my guy friends that truly gets me. I tell him many times that he is like the older pain in the ass brother that I never wanted. I do love him like a brother and consider him part of my family. I don't say that very often about people that come into my life. Most of the time I'll give you the hairy eyeball and keep my distance until I feel comfortable approaching you.

    So, now I want to tell you a funny story as well, so here goes. Once again it was one of those days when some of the boys decided to stay up all night. They were having too much fun to bother with sleep. One of our friends turned in early as he needed to catch an early flight back home. He said goodnight and goodbye to everyone and turned in for the night. So the next morning, I think it was around 5:00 am or so, he came downstairs expecting not to see anyone.

He was thinking that they all finally went to bed, well that wasn't the case! He hears some people talking in the kitchen, walks in and sees them going through the refrigerator for some more lasagna. He said to them, "You guys still up?" And someone replied, "Want some lasagna"? They all busted out laughing. I can just about imagine the surprise look on his face, I am sure it was priceless.

One of my all-time favorite stories is about our friend who rented a car to get around town while he was here. The day came for him to return the car and as we were saying our goodbyes in the front of our house, when our dog Shelby, who loved to be around people, and for some reason took a liking to him, decided to get in the car with him and sit on the center console. Shelby looks at him like OK boss, take me for a ride. She loved car rides, I was laughing so hard as she sat for a good five minutes waiting for her ride. I took a picture of the two of them, and to this day it's still one of my favorites from all the pictures that I have taken throughout the years. I still miss Shelby. She was a really good dog.

I have a lot of good memories of our "Shoootaplooza's." through the years and have the pictures too. I would like to say that I captured a few good moments along the way. These are just some of the memories that I have shared with you. I hope that someday in the future we can have a reunion. One thing I do remember the most is there was always a lot of laughter that filled our home on those long weekends. Good food, good conversation, good friends, and good memories. Times like that those will never last, so if you get the chance, go for it! Make a memory and make it a good one.

The best part I think of all these gatherings are the friends that we made along the way. I can only imagine for those of you that haven't done or experienced something like this, you must think I'm bat shit crazy! Hey, let's meet some people on YouTube that we became friends with, and pick a location say our home, to meet in person and have a fun long weekend yeah.... I don't really know them all that well so there's that. Just typing the sentence gives me the giggles. Yep, we took a chance and it paid off. Which proves to me it doesn't matter where you come from or how you were raised or even how you live your life, there is that possibility of coming together because of one common interest. I wish more people could learn to get along with one another. The world would be a better place. I can honestly say that good times were had by all. So, boys and girls that is a bit of my behind the "Shootapalooza" scenes if you will. Now time to get back to the first part of the story which is Ed and Jules.

So now Ed and Jules are going to meet us in the backyard of our home where the rest of our friends are hanging out. Eric sees that Ed has a beer in his hand. Eric goes over there and knocks it out of his hand, and it lands on the ground. He looks like you just kicked his puppy dog, followed by a look of confusion. Eric reaches into the cooler and hands him "a good beer." Without a word, Ed takes it and then walks over where everyone else is sitting to say hello. Many times in the past, after our "Shootapalooza's" Eric would be doing a Google chat with Ed, I would pop in to say hi and ask him, "Ed what are you drinking?" And he would say. "Two Hearted Ale", as he held up his bottle of beer. He loved that beer; it was his favorite. So, about two years back when Jules was visiting us, we decided to go to the beer store and get some, 'Two Hearted Ale' and do a toast in remembrance of Ed. Jules and I both drank some of that beer, but I got to tell you, it's the worst tasting beer I have ever had in my whole entire life! OK, so I'm not a beer drinker, just letting you know. I also need to confess that Jules didn't care for it either. Every time Eric and I go to the beer store and see that beer, I just smile, and I think of Ed. After everyone got to say hello it was time for dinner. Jules asked me if she could help with anything, and I said yes. I'm not going to turn down any offer for help, just saying. So, as she was helping me in the kitchen, Ed and the other guys were just hanging out having a good time. One thing I can say about Ed and Jules is that they never overstayed their welcome. Most nights, they were the first to leave, they would go back to their hotel and then meet us in the morning for breakfast. The time would go by so fast. Before you know it was time to say goodbye. We said our goodbyes and talk about the plans for the next year when we could all get together again.

A short time after that, Ed couldn't make it to the "Shootapalooza". He was diagnosed with lung cancer. Here's where it gets real for me. My nonna had Non-Hodgkin's Lymphoma. I watched her go through the process of treatment and several years later, it came back. Seeing her go from someone who was strong physically and mentally for her age, to someone who looked weak and frail, broke my heart. I hated seeing her that way. It was extremely hard on me as I live in the United States, and she lived in Canada. There weren't too many times that I was able to take the trip to see her. This wasn't just hard on me, but the whole family as well. I think I understand better than most how cancer can profoundly affect your loved ones.

I remember the time that we were all in the Google chat together, first it was just Eric an Ed. Later, I came into the room to say hi, but noticed that the atmosphere was quite different this time. Jules was also there with Ed which wasn't unusual, but she was noticeably quiet this time. He then told us he had cancer. Not trying to take away anything from Ed but both Eric and I can understand this as we have been up close and personal with this issue as well. The one thing about cancer is it doesn't discriminate. It doesn't care if you're young, old, black, white, gay, straight, rich or poor. Sometimes it seems like there's no escaping it, no matter who you are. So, we continued to talk to Ed and Jules. I have to say I can understand how Jules must have felt. Getting the news about your spouse having cancer, well let's just say it will wreck your whole freaking day and then some. That was the night that we had a lengthy discussion with them. I think it was extremely hard for Ed to be open and to let other people in, as far as I could tell he didn't like talking about his cancer, as I know he was one of those people that never wanted to be the center of attention or spotlight put on him. At that moment in time, my mind was going in many different directions after he told us about his cancer. It was awful hard just to sit there and listen, but it's what we did. It's how we could support them in their moment of crisis. I know that Eric kept in touch with Ed throughout his whole process with his cancer. Eric would update me as to what was happening with Ed's treatments, progress and any other questions or concerns that I had. This part of his life is exceedingly difficult to talk about. I believe this was the time when Jules and I were talking quite a bit back and forth also. For me personally, it was awfully hard to stay positive and give positive support knowing full and well that there was the possibility that he might not survive this, and when that thought occurs you just realize how fragile life really can be. At some point in time, Ed decided to make a video and put it on his YouTube channel to let everyone know that he had cancer and what his status was. He wasn't so worried about himself but wanted us all to focus on another YouTuber who was going through cancer at the same time and was genuinely concerned for him and his family. Ed thought they really needed help at that point in time. He wanted people to help them and not worry about him because he will be ok.

      That to me, is just another example of Ed's graciousness. He always seemed to put other people ahead of himself. He never ceased to amaze me with his kindness and his generosity for family and friends. I am sure there were plenty of times where he felt down and out, or even defeated while dealing with his cancer. What really amazed me was his inner strength to carry on and continue the journey. When mortality comes knocking on your door, you never know how you're going to answer it. I can only imagine there were several times where he had questions as to whether he was going to make it through this process. Cancer is a hard road, and it is not for the faint of heart. I think anytime you go through a situation where you receive really devastating news, which is hard to digest and accept, all you can do is try to move on from it. It's times like those that you realize just what you are made of. The one positive that I can say through all of this, is that you really know who your friends and family are that will support you through whatever issue it is you are having. Let's face it, we're all human beings and we all feel very vulnerable when something like this happens. People in general never want to show vulnerability because they believe that that equals weakness. Truly it is not the case, there are times in your life that bring you to a point of having to ask for help or support from your family or friends. By no means is this something to ever feel ashamed of. We are all human; we all have our trials and tribulations throughout our whole life. I believe some of those are purposely put in our path as a way of learning and growing. That is if we pay attention. I realized that there are times in life where it is hard to look and find the positive. Especially when you're in that negative moment.

I am sure that Jules and Ed had many conversations about his cancer. I would imagine that most of the conversations talked about the concerns, the plans of what to do and when to do it. I can only imagine for both, that this was a very emotional time. Let's face it, you're in uncharted waters and when it comes to cancer you just never know what will happen. Dealing with the uncertainty would be enough to drive anyone crazy. All I can say is thank goodness for Google chat. I am glad that Eric and I got a chance to chat quite a bit with both throughout the whole process of his chemo and other treatments.

That reminds me of a funny little story that I want to share with you. So, there was this one time when Eric, Ed and some of the other guys were in a chat. It was just a regular night of them flapping their gums and nothing major, now Ed's Internet wasn't the greatest. There have been times when they were in the middle of a chat and his Internet would shut down on him or it would freeze, or we couldn't hear what he was saying. So, the running joke was to tell Ed every time that that happened, he needed to upgrade from dial-up. This one time when we lost him in a chat he popped out and popped back in again. He then said something along the lines of "Sorry for the delay, I had Jules up on the roof trying to dial in a better signal for our Internet". Everybody that was in the chat that day was laughing their butts off. I love the fact that he always found humor in everything, even when he was being made fun of. Through it all, I was glad to see he kept his sense of humor. Sometimes you just need to laugh. That is one of the lessons I take away from that.

As I sit here writing this, it makes me pause to reflect on everything that we were a part of these past few years. Some things will stick with me forever because of the situation and circumstances that have a lasting impression. As I would imagine, all of you had your fair share of those moments as well. They have a way of staying with you. One of the things I will never forget is the time when Jules called me to let me know Ed was in the hospital. I believe it wasn't too long after he returned to work and had just finished his chemo treatments. For some reason he wasn't feeling well, so they decided to keep him in the hospital for observation until they could determine exactly what they needed to do, if anything. Maybe something needed to be done or some action to be taken. It wasn't very clear. So, for the most part the phone calls started out on a good note. Jules was confident that they would figure this out and that he would get better and return home. Hopefully, in a reasonable amount of time. I said I hope they get it figured out and please update me if anything changes. A few days later she had called me to let me know that Ed had taken a turn for the worse. She was really hoping that he was going to get better and come out of this ok. The way she was talking as I was listening; I thought the chance of him surviving this has gone down a great deal. I didn't say anything to her, as much as I wanted to, I knew in that moment of time that she was in denial of the possibility of losing him, and she was grabbing on to hope for dear life. If you have ever been in a situation like that, you know exactly what I am talking about. You so desperately want for the person that you love and care about to get better in that moment. You were praying to God, you were doing all kinds of things, and trying to say just about anything, trying to find some positive resolution to hold onto, which unfortunately never comes. Especially in this situation such as Ed's. After getting off the phone with Jules, I gave Eric the update. I hate delivering bad news. God knows I've had my fair share of making most of those types of phone calls or having those kinds of conversations with family and friends.

  The next phone call came a day or two later from Jules, she was letting me know that Ed had passed. It was an incredibly sad day to realize that we had lost one of our good friends. I don't need to tell you what that feels like. There were many phone calls between me and Jules after Ed's passing. I tried to give her as much good sound vice as possible when I was asked. When they say that timing is everything, in this case, it was just all wrong. The days following Ed's passing were awfully hard on her. She lost her husband, and her kids lost a father. This is where grief is different for everyone, in those moments, it's extremely hard to make any decisions. There were several times over the course of that first week that I spoke to her as she asked for advice and I gave it. I tried not to overstep my bounds with certain things that we spoke about, but I also wanted her to be able to make good choices that would benefit her, especially now that she is alone. Don't get me wrong she has kids, but they are all married, and they have family and responsibilities of their own. So, there's only so much that they can do to assist her with all of this. She was just trying to do the best she could in the moment and let me tell you, it was a very tough one for her. When all of this was going on, it really did take me back to Wendy and how she had to work through her grief process as well.

That's the thing about reflection, you never know when it's going to creep into your mind and start those thoughts turning all over again. It takes just that one moment or that one trigger. Seeing my friends dealing with their pain and grief for loved ones lost, this the one thing we can all relate to in some way. The pain that comes knowing that your loved one is gone and they're never coming back. I know, I have lost a lot of family throughout the years all before the age of 45. My mom, my noona, my father-in-law and mother-in-law from a previous marriage, my uncle, my cousin Robbie, and my nonna. All whom I was really close to. So, I can say without a doubt that loss of any kind really sucks! Once you get to a place where you can really accept that they are gone and hard as it may be, you must get on with life. I believe this is the time you really start to heal. Life then becomes different in the sense that you must make new routines and memories without them. When that form of reality hits, it really slaps you in the face and hard! At first, it's exceedingly difficult to have a life without that loved one, but as time goes on you learn how to navigate new paths without them. The negative depressed feelings dwindle. Don't get me wrong they will never be forgotten, they will always have a place in your heart and because they have a place in your heart that is something to give you the strength to go on. To get up every single day and go through your routine of work or whatever your day is now, you somehow just do it. As time goes on you end up having more good days than bad. The other thing that always tends to stay with me, at least in my mind, is the date of one's passing, that date for Ed is October 16th, 2018. It's going to be three years this fall that we have been without Ed and the time seems to have gone by both slow and fast if that makes any sense at all. For both Eric and myself, we can honestly say that Ed's friendship is one to be cherished and to be remembered. I am glad to have been able to have the time that I did with him and to be able to call him a friend of mine. I know Eric feels the same way. I think that there is a huge lesson in all of this to speak about. First of all, as the saying goes, we shouldn't take anything for granted, is true. Keep the people that matter the most to us and let the rest go, and we should live our lives to the fullest. I know it is easier said than done. As I am typing this it makes me think of my mom always said, ""Life is what you make of it". It's true, life is not a game you don't get a do over. You only get this one life, this one moment, this one chance. Make it the best possible one. Enjoy the small moments, the small triumphs, and moments of happiness. Be kind to yourself and others and learn how to be in the moment. Enjoy that moment because those moments turn into memories and that is all we have. They will come, and they will go like a blink of an eye. Forget the bad times and remember the good times. Learn to forgive and forget, to move on and always be moving forward. Tell the people you care about that you love them and do it every day, better yet show them. Remember we only have this moment. All this will come in time so practice patience. That is my takeaway from all of this #BeLikeEd. We love you Ed and we miss you always.

    Writing this book has been quite the journey for me. To put this all out there, you can't even begin to imagine, it is no easy task. It has been one hell of a ride so far, to me it very much felt like a hockey game and not just any hockey game but playing for the Stanley Cup. I'd like to say great game but I'm still in the third period heading down the homestretch. There are quite a few minutes left on the clock. Speaking of hockey, I want to tell you that my favorite hockey player is Wayne Gretzky. One of my favorite quotes from him is, "You miss 100% of the shots you don't take."

Boys and girls that this is the reason why, when I was asked by David to write this book I said yes. It really was an opportunity I couldn't pass up and I hope that all of you reading this will have your own personal take away from this and if not, well then it wasn't time for you to hear my truth and that's OK too. Here is a random thought. Can you imagine trying to play hockey when you're drunk? You're thinking about that one. I know you're laughing.

My part of this journey is almost over, me telling you about Ed and Jules is coming to an end. Unfortunately, the journey that Jules and Wendy, is still going on and it is one that will continue for them both, for years to come. I see so much progress in Wendy and I am so proud of her. She had a lot of hurdles to overcome and she's taking her own path and making a new life for herself and her kids. She is a wonderful mom, and I couldn't have asked for a better friend. As for Jules, I am proud of her too. She is just starting her process of making her new way of life without Ed. I am confident that she will get there too, and she will find her path. It will take time. She is a great friend too. Both my girlfriends are smart, kind, generous and strong women. Life can try to put an obstacle in their way, and they will find a way to go around it or overcome it. They both have a good amount of determination no matter what and I will always be there for them. Besides whom else will go to concerts with me no matter how old I am? That would be Wendy. We may have gray hair and wrinkles, but we will rock on! Banger sisters forever! That's what we say. Hell yeah! I will always love cooking in the kitchen with Jules and she has some kick ass recipes from her homeland and one day I hope to visit there too. Of course, when we cook, wine is a must……for drinking, not cooking! Just sayn. I will be seeing Jules this summer as I invited her to our home for a visit. I am looking forward to the opportunity to spend time with her.

This year has been one of change, growth and opportunity for me. So far, it's been interesting and I'm not sure what the future holds. I guess I will do as I have always done, just roll with it. You never know what will happen or when. Now this is the end my friends and I think that's a line from one of the Doors songs. Don't remember the name of it. Oh boy this truly is turning into what we call a Minnesota goodbye. It always takes a long time to say goodbye. Somehow the conversation keeps going and then it's, "We really should get going!" And then it's more talking and then it's one more final goodbye. I do want to say one more thing. I know I am being a bit chatty at this point. Yep, I'm going to keep writing for another minute or two. I wanted to say thank you David for this opportunity. It has been quite the journey. I want to say thank you to Eric for your support and understanding while I focused on this book. I am glad I took this chance, and I did it.

Eric and I will always remember Ed and he is deeply missed by a lot of people that he has touched. We all have our memories of him as to what he did, who he helped and overall, who he was as a person. All I can say is cherish the time with your family and friends. As I write this, I just found out another friend of ours, Ross from Scotland is not doing very well health wise, and he currently is in the hospital. I am not sure how much time that he has left. As I write my final words, I just learned that Ross passed away May 29, 2021. Rest in peace my friend. This makes these last few sentences all that more important. Make each day the best it can be. Life is truly short, so make some memories and make some really freaking awesome ones! So, if you are one of the fortunate people that makes it to old age, and you are sitting in your rocking chair reflecting on your life overall, it should make you smile and hopefully you have no regrets about the life you have lived. Remember to be gracious. Remember to #BeLikeEd.

GOD BLESS THE UNITED STATES OF AMERICA

To contact the author, David J Brown please visit:
djbrownbooks@gmail.com
To order signed copies of David's five novels:
"Daddy Had to Say Goodbye"
"Flesh of A Fraud"
"Harvest Season"
"Altered Egos"
"#BeLikeEd"
Please visit David's website
@www.davidjbrownbooks.com

You may also request Mr. Brown to speak at your upcoming events @dbrown624@gmail.com

PRINTED IN THE UNITED STATES OF AMERICA

Made in the USA
Monee, IL
27 June 2021